Essential Law for SQE1

Series editor: Wendy Laws

Essential Law for SQE1 is a series of concise textbooks aligned to the latest SQE1 curriculum. Providing candidates with an accessible summary of the core principles in each area of law, the style of each book is precise, with bullet-point lists summarizing key information and revision points concluding each chapter. The books also feature multiple choice questions with answers, example problem questions and a glossary of key cases.

Essential Tort Law for SQE1
Wendy Laws

Essential Dispute Resolution for SQE1
Ben Waters

Essential Business Law and Practice for SQE1
Bill Davies

Essential Land Law for SQE1
Mohammad Sabuj

Essential Legal System and Legal Services for SQE1
Ian Bowden and Zaman F. Kala

Essential Criminal Law and Criminal Practice for SQE1
James Thornton, Amanda Parker and Orla Slattery

Essential Constitutional and Administrative Law for SQE1
Zaman F. Kala and Ian Bowden

For more information about this series, please visit: www.routledge.com/

Essential Constitutional and Administrative Law for SQE1

Essential Constitutional and Administrative Law for SQE1 explains key principles of the UK constitution, the organs of the state, judicial review, as well as retained EU law/assimilated law, in a clear, concise, and easy-to-understand style. The use of practical examples allows such key principles to be effectively introduced and illustrated. It demonstrates the importance of the system of supremacy and the rule of law and how the concept of separation of powers ensures effective governance, including an understanding of human rights legislation and public order law.

The book provides a clear and structured approach with opportunities to apply the relevant principles to the law. The book also includes a range of interactive features including:

- Revision points: Each chapter concludes with a concise list of key revision points.
- Multiple Choice Questions: Each section of the book provides multiple choice questions following the SQE1 question format (with answers to enable you to test your knowledge).

Further multiple choice questions and answers are also provided on the companion website.

Part of a series of books aimed at those who are preparing for SQE1, this concise and accessible text provides a clear understanding of the key principles of the essential constitutional and administrative law and will enable you to test your assessment skills.

Zaman F. Kala is a lecturer and accredited mediator in the School of Law and Policing at the University of Central Lancashire, where he teaches on the undergraduate and postgraduate programmes. Prior to embarking upon a career in academia, Zaman worked as a fee earner at a leading firm of solicitors, specialising in insurance litigation and dispute resolution.

Ian Bowden is a practising solicitor advocate with many years of experience working in legal practice. He is also a senior teaching fellow at Liverpool John Moores University. Ian has experience across a wide range of practice areas including civil litigation, employment law, wills and probate, and medical negligence. He also trains students in the key skills of advocacy, interviewing, advising, and legal research.

Zaman and Ian are the authors of *Essential Legal System and Legal Services for SQE1*.

Essential Constitutional and Administrative Law for SQE1

Zaman F. Kala and Ian Bowden

Routledge
Taylor & Francis Group
LONDON AND NEW YORK

Designed cover image: Getty Images

First published 2025
by Routledge
4 Park Square, Milton Park, Abingdon, Oxon OX14 4RN

and by Routledge
605 Third Avenue, New York, NY 10158

Routledge is an imprint of the Taylor & Francis Group, an informa business

British Library Cataloguing-in-Publication Data
A catalogue record for this book is available from the British Library

Library of Congress Cataloging-in-Publication Data
Names: Kala, Zaman F., author. | Bowden, Ian, author.
Title: Essential constitutional & administrative law for SQE1 / Zaman F. Kala and Ian Bowden.
Other titles: Essential constitutional and administrative law for SQE1
Description: Abingdon, Oxon [UK] ; New York, NY : Routledge, 2024. | Series: Routledge -essential law for SQE1 | Includes index.
Identifiers: LCCN 2024036870 | ISBN 9781032641997 (hardback) | ISBN 9781032641942 (paperback) | ISBN 9781032642024 (ebook)
Subjects: LCSH: Constitutional law—Great Britain—Examinations, questions, etc. | Administrative law—Great Britain—Examinations, questions, etc. | Rule of law—Great Britain—Examinations, questions, etc. | Separation of powers—Great Britain—Examinations, questions, etc. | Judicial review—Great Britain—Examinations, questions, etc. | International and municipal law—Great Britain—Examinations, questions, etc. | Law—Great Britain—Examinations, questions, etc. | Solicitors Qualifying Examination. | Great Britain. Human Rights Act 1998. | LCGFT: Study guides.
Classification: LCC KD3930 .K35 2024 | DDC 342.41—dc23/eng/20240812
LC record available at https://lccn.loc.gov/2024036870

ISBN: 978-1-032-64199-7 (hbk)
ISBN: 978-1-032-64194-2 (pbk)
ISBN: 978-1-032-64202-4 (ebk)

DOI: 10.4324/9781032642024

Typeset in The Sans
by Apex CoVantage, LLC

Access the SQE1 Series Companion Website: www.routledge.com/cw/sqe

For every colleague and every student that ever inspired us that we had something to say. Our thanks to Iesha Toussena, Simeon Todorov, and Chris O'Rourke for helping to choose the cover image.

Contents

Table of Cases

Table of Statutes

Introduction

This book provides a clear, concise explanation of key principles of constitutional and administrative law. Its focus is on those areas which fall within the assessment specification for the **Solicitors Qualifying Examination Part 1 Functioning Legal Knowledge** ('SQE1').

In so doing, it also covers the areas of public law central to most undergraduate public law modules. Although the book does mention the role of EU law, this is limited to the place that EU law now holds within the UK constitution.

The style of the book reflects the SQE1 assessment specification:

- The SQE1 assessment requires knowledge and understanding of fundamental legal principles and the ability to apply them.
- Candidates are not required to recall specific case names or statutory provisions (except where they are normally used in practice to describe a legal principle).
- Candidates will be tested on the current law and will not be tested on the historical development of the law.

In order to reflect these requirements, the book explains the current key principles of public law in a clear, easy to follow style. Principles are introduced and illustrated by reference to realistic factual examples. References to key cases and statutes are provided.

This approach enables the book to provide a fluent narrative account of key principles which is clear and accessible, making it easier for the reader to understand the principles, remember them, and apply them in an assessment.

Key Features to Assist Learning

Revision points: Each chapter concludes with a concise list of key revision points.

Multiple choice questions: The SQE1 assessment uses multiple choice questions to test understanding of key principles. Multiple choice questions, following the SQE format, are provided at the end of each section of the book (with answers at the end of the book).

DOI: 10.4324/9781032642024-1

PART 1 The UK Constitution

1 Introduction to the United Kingdom Constitution

Constitutional and administrative law, often referred to as public law, is the area of law that governs how the government and the institutions of government interact with the wider public. In essence, public law regulates how the government uses its role and powers.

Public law is a vital aspect of everyday life as it helps to mitigate the unequal relationship that exists between the government and the general public. The government holds a unique position in that the operation of government itself requires that decisions be made that amend, add, or remove the rights of individuals. It is therefore essential that individuals have the right to ensure that the government acts within the law. A citizen can ask for judicial review if they are unhappy with a decision of an authoritative body.

Legal professionals who operate in the area of public law can specialise in various areas including constitutional/administrative law, tax law, judicial review, and criminal law.

1.1 SQE1 Syllabus

The SQE1 syllabus requires that an individual has an awareness of a wide range of constitutional and administrative topics. These include an understanding of parliament and process, government accountability, and constitutional conventions. In this first chapter we will set the scene regarding each of these areas with a view to ensuring that the reader has context on which to build as they progress through the text.

1.2 Chapter Overview

Within this chapter we will evaluate the notion of constitution and will look at how constitutions come into existence and the unique position created by the UK's approach to constitution as a principle.

DOI: 10.4324/9781032642024-3

The chapter will consider the sources and classification of the UK constitution and will contrast this with alternative approaches to how nations look to confer and communicate the relationship and rights that flow between states and citizens.

1.3 What Is a Constitution?

The term constitution is used in a variety of contexts to outline the rules and principles by which an organisation is to be governed. This could be anything from a working men's club to a sports team through to a political party or a nation.

In public law terms, a constitution outlines the principles and rules by which a nation organises its own governance and systems of controls. In essence, it is a rule book for the nation that describes the institutions of the state and the often complex relationships between the institutional players and the citizens of the country.

In addition, the constitution delineates the powers that the state holds and balances these with the rights available to an individual.

It is important to note that there is not one fixed definition of what actually makes a constitution or what the constitution must cover. This is a very flexible process.

In the next sections, we will look at the written and unwritten constitutions and how the United Kingdom's own unique constitution is formed.

1.4 Written and Unwritten Constitutions

Constitutions are typically divided into two variations – they are either written constitutions or unwritten constitutions. As the names suggest, in one format we are presented with a formal written document that comprehensively outlines the supreme law of the land, as well as detailing the rights and responsibilities of the government. The oldest written constitution is that of the United States of America. This was drafted in September 1787, ratified on 21 June 1788 and came into force on 4 March 1789.

By contrast, an unwritten constitution, whilst serving the same purpose, does this without having the single constitutional document at its heart. Instead, the unwritten constitution is based upon a collection of laws, customs, and precedents.

Unwritten constitutions are often found in countries with strong legal traditions and a long history, such as New Zealand, Israel, and the United Kingdom.

The UK's constitution has no single authoritative written document that outlines how the government and parliament should operate. Instead, the UK constitution is drawn from a variety of different sources.

1.5 Sources of the United Kingdom Constitution

The UK constitution cannot be found in a single document or even in one of two places. Instead, it is made up from a variety of different sources. There are four principal sources to consider:

1) Acts of Parliament
2) Case Law
3) The Royal Prerogative; and
4) Constitutional Conventions.

It is important to ensure a working knowledge of each of these sources to understand the constitution as a whole.

1.5.1 Legal Sources

1.5.1.1 Acts of Parliament

A range of primary legislation enacted by the UK Parliament form aspects of the UK constitution. The starting point for considering the legislative aspects of the UK constitution would be Magna Carta (1215).

MAGNA CARTA

Magna Carta (translated as Great Charter) was an agreement reached at Runnymede in 1215 between King John and the English barons who had previously rebelled against the King. The charter guaranteed certain rights to 'freemen of the realm' including trial by jury.

In chapters 39 and 40 of the charter it is stated:

> 39. No free man shall be seized or imprisoned or stripped of his rights or possessions, or outlawed or exiled, or deprived of his standing in any other way, nor will we proceed with force against him, or send others to do so, except by the lawful judgement of his equals or by the law of the land.
> 40. To no one will we sell, to no one deny or delay right or justice.

Magna Carta placed formal limits on the King's power and brought about the concept that the ruling monarch should not be above the constraints of the law.

In terms of the constitution, Magna Carta could be viewed as the foundation of the constitutional principle of the rule of law, namely that everyone within a state should be bound by and entitled to the benefit of the law.

Although not a formal written constitution, it is a significant point in the journey towards the unwritten constitution that we have today. It could be considered that the charter was an inspiration to many concepts that we consider to be vital today such as 'habeas corpus' – the provision that a person may not be detained without legal reason.

BILL OF RIGHTS (1689)

This act was the key piece of legislation that followed the Glorious Revolution, which saw the virtually bloodless expulsion and abdication of one king (James II) and the installation of another (William III and Mary).

In the Bill of Rights, Parliament asserted the supremacy of Parliament over the King in making laws and in raising taxes.

The Bill of Rights also guaranteed several other key political and civil rights, including free speech (at least for members of Parliament), the right to bear arms (at least for Protestants), and the right to petition the government for grievances.

Although Parliament would remain an institution for the privileged few, the Bill of Rights ensured that they did so in the name of the English people as a whole, and the members of the House of Commons served as elected representatives of local districts. The Bill also ensured that Parliament was required to meet on a regular basis and introduced the concept of free elections.

ACTS OF UNION 1706–1707

The Acts of Union were two Acts of Parliament: the Union with Scotland Act 1706 passed by the Parliament of England and the Union with England Act 1707 passed by the Parliament of Scotland.

The combined effect of the acts was the formalisation of the terms of the Treaty of Union that had been agreed between the countries on 22 July 1706. In essence, the kingdoms of England and Scotland were, in the words of the treaty:

> United into One Kingdom by the Name of Great Britain.

The acts became law on 1 May 1707, and on that date the Scottish and English Parliaments were joined to the Parliament of Great Britain, based in the Houses of Parliament at Westminster.

It should be noted that as well as combining the parliaments, the acts did preserve both the separate Church of Scotland and also the Scottish legal system.

PARLIAMENT ACT 1911

During the early 1900s the House of Lords' power of legislative veto was becoming problematic for the Commons. This came to a head when the Lords refused to pass David Lloyd-George's 'people's budget' of 1909.

The use of the veto resulted in a general election in 1910, after which the budget finally passed. There was then the need for a second general election that was largely fought on the issue of reforming the upper chamber of Parliament.

This resulted in the Parliament Act 1911, which revoked the House of Lords' power to veto a bill, except one to extend the lifetime of a Parliament. Instead, the Lords could only delay bills. The act also reduced the maximum lifespan of a Parliament from seven years to five years.

PARLIAMENT ACT 1949

The Parliament Act 1949 was introduced to further limit the House of Lords' ability to delay legislation by placing specific requirements on the Lords regarding different types of bills.

POLICE AND CRIMINAL EVIDENCE ACT 1984

The Police and Criminal Evidence Act 1984, often referred to as PACE, governs significant areas of police powers of investigation, including arrest, detention, interrogation, entry and search of premises, personal search, and the taking of samples.

The act is underpinned by the PACE Codes of Practice, which guide police officers when carrying out their roles. The act attempts to strike a fair balance between the exercise of power by those in authority and the rights of members of the public and has significant relevance regarding the civil liberties of the public.

HUMAN RIGHTS ACT 1998

The Human Rights Act 1998 incorporates the European Convention on Human Rights into domestic legislation. The act was a real shift in the protections afforded to citizens in areas including the right to life, the right to respect for private and family life, the right to personal liberty, and the right to a fair trial, amongst others.

There have also been a raft of more recent legislation that has impacted upon the constitution, including the devolution settlements, the European Union (Withdrawal) Act 2018, and the existence of the Supreme Court;

1.5.1.2 Common Law

The UK operates under a 'common law' system, which means that judges declare the law on a case-by-case basis derived through the system of 'custom and precedent'.

Within this area, it is important to note that it is not the role of the courts to make the law, but it is their role to interpret the law. This often results in a form of law creation completed by judges.

It is notable that case law judges have established important features of the UK constitution, such as residual freedom rights, the requirement for state officials' actions to have legal basis, judicial review, statutory interpretation, and the idea that public authorities are subject to limitations and do not possess arbitrary power.

1.5.1.3 The Royal Prerogative

A.V. Dicey defined the royal prerogative as

> the residue of discretionary or arbitrary authority, which at any given time is legally left in the hands of the Crown . . . Every act which the government can lawfully do without the authority of an Act of Parliament is done in virtue of this prerogative.[1]

Prerogative powers have been an aspect of the legal system since the Middle Ages. Previously they were the preserve of the monarch (and hence royal prerogative), but they now remain as powers that are exercised by government ministers. The powers available under the prerogative are multifaceted, with ministers possessing the power to engage in war and to deploy troops; to conduct foreign policy and enter into treaties; to make public and judicial appointments; to issue passports; and to grant state honours.

It is important to note that even with a great deal of the royal prerogative powers now residing with ministers, the monarch is still able to exercise some powers directly. These are known as reserve powers.

The most important of these relate to procedural aspects of government and parliament and include the power to appoint and dismiss ministers; the power to summon and end the current parliamentary session; and the ongoing power to give Royal Assent to bills passed by parliament, effectively giving them legal standing.

Where the powers have been delegated to ministers they are accountable for how the powers are used. Should a prerogative power have been used in an inappropriate fashion then the exercise of powers can be subject to consideration by the relevant court.

1.5.2 Non-Legal Sources

1.5.2.1 Constitutional Conventions

A constitutional convention is a non-legal source within the UK constitution. They are an unwritten understanding about how something in Parliament should be done which, although not legally enforceable, are almost universally observed.

The fact that conventions are non-legal sources of the constitution does not mean that they are ineffective as they are backed up through notions of political, rather than legal, sanction.

1 A. V. Dicey, *Introduction to the Study of the Law of the Constitution*, 10th edn. (London: MacMillan, 1959), 424.

The use of conventions is a product of accepted custom and practice within the political process, as an example where a Prime Minister loses a vote of confidence within the House of Commons, it is accepted that the PM's resignation will follow.

However, it would be incorrect to assume that conventions are merely a matter for Parliament; they are in fact at work across a wide swathe of government branches, be that the legislative, the judicial, or the executive.

In constitutional terms, they play a vital role due to the inherent flexibility that is built into the convention system. As an example, one established convention is that the House of Lords will not normally veto secondary legislation. The most important word here being the use of 'normally', which indicates a degree of flexibility showing that conventions have different levels of requirement to comply.

They are evolutionary in nature and serve to limit the powers of the monarch through a system of control that does not require major changes to the constitution. They also have the effect of holding the government accountable to the Houses of Parliament for the decisions and actions that they take.

IMPORTANT CONSTITUTIONAL CONVENTIONS

It can be helpful to consider a number of common constitutional conventions as a means to understand how they work within the constitution as a whole.

1) As found in the Cabinet Manual, 'the Sovereign should not be drawn into party politics, and if there is doubt it is the responsibility of those involved in the political process, and in particular the parties represented in parliament, to seek to determine and communicate clearly to the Sovereign who is best placed to be able to command the confidence of the House of Commons'.
2) The government will always put bills before the monarch and advise that the bill has passed both Houses of Parliament.
3) The prerogative powers of the monarch will be exercised by, or on the advice of, ministers with all ministerial communications with the Sovereign remaining confidential.
4) All ministers that comprise the government of the day are jointly responsible for the government's decisions and policies under the convention of collective ministerial responsibility.
5) The House of Commons has primacy over the House of Lords.
6) Devolved matters will be for the devolved assembly to legislate upon, unless the devolved assembly has consented for the UK Parliament to legislate on the matter at hand.
7) The government must uphold the independence of the judiciary and members of the judiciary will not play an active political role.

1.6 Classification of the United Kingdom Constitution?

Constitutions are frequently classified according to a range of different characteristics. As we have seen, we have written and unwritten constitutions, but we also have a number of other methods of classification. We shall consider some of these in turn.

1.6.1 Flexible or Inflexible

It is possible as part of the design of the constitution to include a distinctive requirement for either flexibility or rigidity.

Flexible constitutions are identifiable by an adaptable approach that is simple to amend as circumstances require. This allows for societal change, technological advancement, or changes in the administrative basis of a nation to be quickly reflected within the constitutional settlement. The process of incorporating flexibility, into the constitutional system, is achieved by ensuring that amendments can be simply introduced and enacted.

Flexibility is often a key requirement for developing nations to use as they allow the system to flex as the nation rapidly grows. They are also vital as they ensure that the complexity of the constitution meets the stage of development of the nation.

Inflexible or rigid constitutions are more fixed in nature and are identifiable by a much more onerous process for amendment. They suffer through their inability to change to meet societal needs, whilst also having the strength that comes from a set, agreed approach that does not change with the weather.

Rigid approaches tend to be viewed as sacred documents that are a part of a nation's identity. They provide stability and demonstrate consistency and permanence.

1.6.2 Unitary and Federal

Constitutions can be classified on the basis of being either unitary or federal.

Under a unitary constitution, such as that found in the United Kingdom, decision-making power is largely centralised around the Houses of Parliament. Although it could be argued that post devolution, it should perhaps be considered as a quasi-federal constitutional arrangement.

Federal systems entail power residing at both a centralised national level and also within an identified lower level. An example of this would be the United States of

America, where there is a central government role that is aligned with power devolved to each state to make laws on a state-by-state basis.

1.6.3 Parliamentary and Presidential

Constitutions can also be considered in terms of being either parliamentary or presidential.

In a parliamentary constitutional approach, the Prime Minister, as head of the executive branch of government, will be the individual who has responsibility for the actions of the government. An example of this would be the United Kingdom where the Prime Minister holds the power with the monarch holding a largely symbolic role.

Where a presidential approach is taken, the president will be both the head of state (akin to the monarch) but will also be the head of the executive branch of government. As can be viewed in the United States, despite the two facets to the role, the president is not a member of the legislature and so is not directly accountable to that body.

Chapter 1 Revision Points

This chapter has introduced a range of concepts within the area of constitution with a view to assisting the reader to understand how the various processes and roles provide an interconnected network, upon which the processes that we will consider in the upcoming chapters are used.

We have observed that the UK constitution is unwritten and uncodified and cannot therefore be viewed within a single document or source. Instead the UK constitution is made up of a number of components including statute, case law, the royal prerogative and through constitutional conventions.

Multiple Choice Questions

Question 1

The government wishes to introduce legislation that will compensate victims of coastal erosion.

Which of the following options provides the best description of the approaches available to the government in relation to using royal prerogative?

A. The government cannot introduce the scheme, using prerogative powers, as they do not have statutory authority to do so.
B. The government may use prerogative powers to adopt a non-statutory compensation scheme which would avoid the issue of statutory authority. This would be sufficient as long as it is approved by Parliament.
C. The government, under constitutional conventions, can use statutory powers rather than prerogative powers to introduce the scheme.
D. Prerogative powers can be used to introduce the scheme as long as the compensation offered is equal to or less than any statutory scheme that is already in existence.
E. The government will be able to adopt a non-statutory scheme and raise funds pursuant to its powers under the royal prerogative.

Question 2

The government's new Fictional Act 2023, if introduced, would be a clear breach of a recognised constitutional convention.

Which of the following best describes the constitutional implications of introducing legislation in breach of a constitutional convention?

A. Where an Act of Parliament is a clear breach of a recognised constitutional convention, the legislation would simply be struck down by the Supreme Court.
B. The new law will be applied by the courts who have a duty to apply the law and to disregard the constitutional convention.
C. The new law will be applied by the courts who will disregard the constitutional convention, if the breach of the convention meets the reasonableness test.
D. The existing constitutional convention will prevent the government from introducing the new legislation if it is clearly a breach of established procedure.
E. Whilst courts will recognise that a constitutional convention is in play, it is their role to apply the legislation as passed by Parliament.

Question 3

The government's new Fictional Act 2023 has passed through all stages in Parliament and has been submitted to the King for Royal Assent. However, a national pressure group claims that the bill breaches established international law and the King should therefore refuse to give Royal Assent.

Will the act be refused Royal Assent?

A. Yes, the King is unable to give Royal Assent to legislation that breaches existing law.
B. Yes, the King is unable to give Royal Assent to legislation that breaches international law.
C. Yes, as the King could face legal sanction should he grant Royal Assent to legislation that breaches international law.
D. No, because by constitutional convention the King always grants Royal Assent to a bill that has passed through all stages in Parliament.
E. No, because by law the King must always grant Royal Assent to a bill that has passed through all stages in Parliament.

PART 2 Core Institutions of the State

2 Constitutional Institutions and Roles

A constitutional institution, constitutional body, or constitutional organ is simply an institution of government that is created under the auspices of the constitution itself.

2.1 SQE1 Syllabus

The SQE1 syllabus requires that an individual has an awareness of a wide range of constitutional and administrative topics. These include an understanding of the institutions, and interactions between institutions, that ensure the operation of the administration of government. In this chapter we will look in detail at the main institutions of the state from Parliament and government through to the Crown and the judiciary.

2.2 Chapter Overview

Within this chapter we will evaluate the institutions of the state and will look at how institutions have come into existence, how they hold the authority to govern, and how they interact within the unique structure of the UK constitution.

The chapter will consider the roles that exist within the constitution upon which power and control rests. We will also consider notions of accountability, privilege, and power.

2.3 United Kingdom Constitutional Institutions

The constitutional institutions of modern government are Parliament, the judiciary, the executive, the civil service, regional governments, public authorities with policy implementation powers, and local government. In this section, we shall review a number of these in turn.

DOI: 10.4324/9781032642024-5

2.3.1 Legislative Power

Legislative power is simply the power to make and amend laws. In the UK this requires consideration of Parliament, the legislative process, and the concept of parliamentary privilege.

2.3.1.1 The UK Parliament

The UK Parliament comprises three central and intertwined elements – the House of Commons, the House of Lords, and the Monarchy.

The main functions of the UK Parliament are to:

- Hold the government accountable by checking and challenging government actions.
- Following government placing legislation before Parliament, Parliament has the role of passing new laws and amending existing laws.
- Debating the issues of the day.
- The approval of government spending plans and providing a check on the use of those funds.
- Providing the personnel who collectively comprise the government of the day. These are drawn typically from the House of Commons, but can be drawn from the House of Lords – as was observed in 2023 with Lord Cameron becoming foreign secretary.

Following the Parliament Acts of 1911 and 1949, the importance of the House of Commons has been supreme over the other two.

THE COMPOSITION OF PARLIAMENT

It is important to understand how Parliament is structured as a means of understanding the legislative process.

THE HOUSE OF COMMONS

The House of Commons is the democratically elected house of the UK Parliament, comprising of 650 Members of Parliament, or MPs.

The Commons is actually the lower house of Parliament.

MPs are elected via general elections, at which the whole of the House will seek re-election at the expiration of the fixed-term parliament or at a time within the fixed term chosen by the government.

MPs can also be elected at by-elections, which are called when a sitting MP's seat becomes available and will be fought on an individual seat basis.

The voting system for selecting MPs to Parliament is referred to as the first past the post system. In essence, the candidate who, in each constituency, receives the most votes is elected as the Member of Parliament for that constituency.

The government and Prime Minister are selected on the basis of which political party has won the most constituencies, with the largest party's leader invited to form a government.

Within the House of Commons, the Speaker of the House is the chair of the Commons and will oversee parliamentary process. The Speaker will be chosen from amongst the Members of Parliament but the role is actually impartial and so the post holder will be expected to remain neutral in completing their role.

THE HOUSE OF LORDS

The House of Lords, although the upper house within the Houses of Parliament, is actually the second chamber of the UK Parliament.

The Lords is made up of unelected representatives. Historically, the Lords was comprised of hereditary peers – these are individuals who are allowed to sit within the Lords by right of birth. The number of hereditary peers was reduced to just 92 peers following the introduction of the House of Lords Act 1999.

In addition to the hereditary peers, the Lords also has a number of life peers, who make up the majority of those who sit on the hallowed red benches. These are appointed by the King, under the Life Peerages Act 1958, on the advice of the Prime Minister.

Currently, there are around 800 members who are eligible to sit within the House. These are made up of the Lords Temporal and the Lords Spiritual.

The Lords Temporal are the secular members of the House of Lords and comprise both hereditary and life peers. The Lords Spiritual are the 26 bishops of the Church of England who are entitled to sit within the Lords.

PARLIAMENTARY MEETING, SESSIONS, SITTINGS, AND DURATION

The whole of the parliamentary process is underpinned by a range of established time requirements that are placed upon the House.

MEETING

As outlined within the Meeting of Parliament Act 1694 (also known as the Triennial Act), it is a requirement that Parliament should hold a 'session' at least once in every three-year period. Although the act has been partly repealed, as part of the Electoral Act 1963 and the Statute Law Revision Act 1867, it is still in force today.

Of course, in practice, Parliament meets throughout the year anyway, due to the volume of work that is required to be completed.

SESSIONS AND SITTINGS

Whilst a 'parliament' is the period of time that elapses between one general election and the next, each parliament is subdivided into several sessions that begin and end in the spring. These sessions are further subdivided into sittings. A sitting is the daily meeting of either the House of Commons or the House of Lords and at the end of each sitting the business of the House is adjourned until the next sitting.

It is possible for a session of Parliament to be ended through the process of prorogation. This terminates all ongoing business of the House, unless an ongoing public bill, by agreement, can be carried forward from one session to the next.

DURATION

Prior to the Parliament Act 1911, the duration of a parliament was limited to a maximum of seven years, under the Septennial Act 1716. However, as part of the sweeping changes to Parliament brought in by the 1911 act, the maximum duration of a parliament was reduced to five years, commencing with the first meeting of Parliament after the election. When the ruling party was seeking to call a general election, the Prime Minister would advise the monarch to use the royal prerogative to affect the election. However, this allowed the ruling party to seek to call elections at times that were most suited to that party regarding their public standing.

It should be noted that the five-year maximum period was a reference to the maximum lifetime of a parliament and was not a specification for the time between general elections taking place. In practice it was rare for the ruling party to wait until such a time, choosing to strike when the maximum advantage was available to their chances of re-election.

This was changed by the Fixed-Term Parliaments Act 2011, which provided for fixed dates when a general election should be held, with there being a five-year period between the election days.

However, in 2019, the Conservative government, seeking to call an election far earlier than the five-year period required under the 2011 act, introduced the Early Parliamentary General Election Act 2019. When this passed with a majority of 438 votes to 20, the 2011 act was clearly redundant legislation.

After the Conservative Party's overwhelming majority at the 2019 election, they put forward legislation to repeal both the 2011 and 2019 acts, returning the question of duration back to the royal prerogative approach that had been used previously.

2.3.1.2 The Legislative Process

It is important, in outlining the legislative process, to firstly consider the types of bills which can be introduced to Parliament.

PUBLIC BILLS

Public bills are proposed changes to the law that impact upon the population in general. Bills that are successful in progressing through Parliament are almost exclusively introduced to Parliament by the government. However, it is important to note that the vast majority of public bills originate from individual backbench MPs. These are termed as private members' bills and are rarely successful in making it from the bill stage through to appearing on the statute book. As an example, in the parliamentary session for 2004–2005, not one private members' bill was passed and in the 2005–2006 session only three were successful.

PRIVATE BILLS

There are two types of private bills that will typically be put before Parliament.

The first type relates to matters that benefit specific individuals, and historically these have related to issues of marriage, divorce, and British nationality.

The second type relates to acts that are for the benefit of organisations – such as extra powers to local authorities, or to authorise major projects such as rail infrastructure.

HYBRID BILLS

Hybrid bills mix the characteristics of both public and private bills and tend to be quite rare. They are generally used as part of the process of securing powers to construct and operate major infrastructure projects of national standing. An example would be the HS2 building programme.

STAGES WITHIN THE LEGISLATIVE PROCESS

Policy Formulation

It is important to note that the process of introducing legislation commences long before a bill is introduced to Parliament. Depending on the type of bill to be introduced, the process can start in a variety of places, with the most common starting point being within a UK government department.

At this stage, it will tend to be that the process of research, evaluation, and policy development will be carried out by officials within a government department at the request of the relevant minister.

THE GOVERNMENT'S LEGISLATIVE PROGRAMME

Prior to the start of each parliamentary session, the government is required to determine the areas in which it is seeking to legislate, and this is then unveiled in the King's Speech at the opening of parliament.

Behind the scenes, government departments must put their proposed bills to the Parliamentary Business and Legislation Cabinet Committee who will assess the necessity, political urgency, and progression of the policy of a wide range of bills. There will then be a series of trade-offs, required to ensure consistency, prior to the creation of the agenda placed before the monarch.

It is typically the case that bills that allow for the delivery of manifesto commitments, or those that are viewed as priorities for the ruling party, are given precedence. It should be noted that any bill that does not make the cut at this stage can be published as a draft bill with a view to then introducing the act at a later session of parliament.

Where a bill is published in draft form, it can be made subject to the process of pre-legislative scrutiny. Where this is used, it is possible for legislation to receive parliamentary input before it is finalised. This process will be completed either via a House of Commons select committee or through the convening of a specific joint committee of members from either the House of Commons or the House of Lords.

The pre-legislative scrutiny model is rarely used in practice, with only 53 bills being put to scrutiny in this manner between June 2007 and December 2022.

PREPARATION FOR PARLIAMENT

Before any bill is introduced into parliament, the content of the bill must be signed off by the relevant cabinet committee. After approval has been given, the bill will then progress to the Office for Parliamentary Counsel, whose legal drafting team will seek to draft the legal wording of the bill. The final wording is then submitted back to the Parliamentary Business and Legislation Cabinet who will check the wording of the bill and will add in any required explanatory notes and impact assessments.

INTRODUCTION TO PARLIAMENT

With the preliminary stages complete, the bill then moves into the formal stage of the process when the bill is introduced into parliament. It should be noted that the formal stage can be commenced either within the Lords or within the Commons.

The Figure 2.1 confirms the process of a bill regardless of whether it commences in the upper or lower house.

In considering the stages of a bill, we will analyse in detail the progression of a bill that starts in the House of Commons.

FIRST READING

The first stage of the bill's progression through parliament is the first reading. This stage is largely one of parliamentary process rather than substantive evaluation of the bill and its contents.

The process commences with the short title of the bill being read out and this, along with the explanatory notes and any other relevant documentation (such as impact assessments), are then published. Within this stage the bill is not debated, and once procedure is satisfied, the bill proceeds to the next stage.

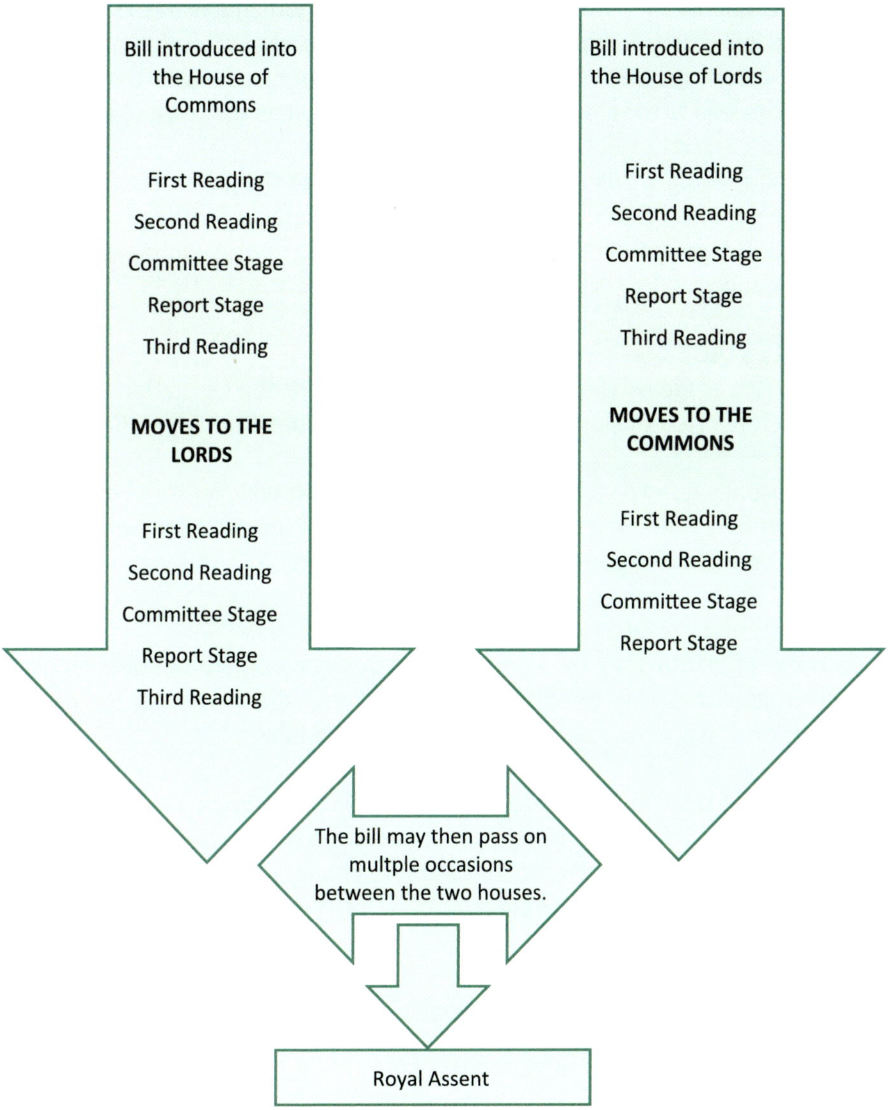

Figure 2.1 Stages within the legislative process

SECOND READING

It is when the bill reaches the second reading stage that the process of parliamentary debate commences. At second reading, parliament is then able to debate the general principles of the bill. The debate provides the government with information on the likely positions that will be taken by the House and in particular opposition parties.

At this stage, it is not possible for the House to amend the bill, but there are a range of steps that can follow.

For example, opposition parties are able to table amendments with the aim of preventing the bill from progressing further. This is rarely successful (the last bill defeated at second reading was the Shops Bill 1986), but it does signal the opposition intent and can lead to the government changing position on the proposed legislation.

After second reading is complete, it is then the role of the government to table a programme's motion that outlines the proposed timetable for the progression of the legislation through parliament. This is voted upon but is almost always successfully passed.

COMMITTEE STAGE

The committee stage is where much of the scrutiny of the legislation takes place and is therefore often the longest stage in a bill's passage through parliament.

The bill is usually referred to a general committee that will consist of between six and 50 members who have been appointed by the Committee of Selection. The selection is made along party lines to ensure that each committee represents the respective division of parties within the House.

The process of scrutiny, by the committee, requires consideration of each clause and schedule with a view to either agreeing the passage, amending the passage, removing the passage, or adding new clauses of schedules.

The outcome of the committee stage will often be amendments to the bill. These could be simple matters of drafting to clarify the text or tidy up clauses through to new proposals from ministers or considerable changes, should there have been new events that require consideration.

REPORT STAGE

The next stage in the process is the Report Stage, at which there is a further opportunity for MPs to influence the bill.

Any MP can propose amendments, new clauses, or new schedules to the bill, and these are then considered by the Speaker of the House who must decide which will be debated and which will be subject to a vote.

It is typical that the Speaker will tend to put forward amendments that have been put forward by the government, amendments put forward by the main opposition, and amendments that have cross-party support.

THIRD READING

With the prior stages complete, the bill then returns to the House for the third reading. At this stage, the amended bill will now be debated. However, it should be noted that this stage is again largely procedural, with debates tending to be less than an hour in duration and this time is often largely taken up by the completion of final votes leading to the approval of the bill at third reading. Again, defeats of bills at this stage are very rare, with the last example being the Local Authority Works (Scotland) Bill 1977.

TRANSFER TO THE HOUSE OF LORDS

Following the third reading in the Commons, the bill then proceeds to the House of Lords for ongoing scrutiny by the upper house.

The procedure in the House of Lords largely mirrors the process of the House of Commons except that the timetable within the Lords is controlled by the Lords themselves, and this can slow down the progress of the bill as peers often seek to provide more detailed scrutiny of the proposed legislation. It is often the case that the committee stage within the Lords is completed by the whole House rather than by a separate committee.

Once the bill has completed the third reading in the Lords, it is then sent back to the Commons for consideration of any amendments that have been made.

In theory, the bill could then move an indefinite number of times between the two Houses until such time as proceedings end due to prorogation. However, in practice, it tends to be the case that should the Commons disagree with the Lords amendments, the Commons will simply resubmit the original wording back to the Lords which the Lords will usually accept.

ROYAL ASSENT

Once the bill has been agreed by both Houses, even if just by procedure rather than on the substantive content, the final stage of the process is Royal Assent.

At this point the bill goes to the monarch, who will officially agree the bill and this then becomes an Act of Parliament. The Act of Parliament takes legal effect either on the day of Royal Assent or on a later date if this is stipulated in the legislation itself.

2.3.1.3 Parliamentary Privilege

The final aspect of legislative power to consider is the notion of parliamentary privilege.

Parliamentary privilege is a set of constitutional law principles which provide certain rights and privileges that allow Parliament to work effectively and independently without interference from the Monarchy, the judiciary, or other external authorities.

As with many aspects of the constitutional basis employed in the UK, it is not possible to reference a single definitive guide as to what constitutes parliamentary privilege. However, the two main privileges are freedom of speech and the right to control the composition and procedures of parliament.

FREEDOM OF SPEECH

Article 9 of the Bill of Rights 1689 states:

> the Freedome of Speech and Debates or Proceedings in Parlyament ought not to be impeached or questioned in any Court or Place out of Parlyament.

This statement enshrines the view that no other authority, including a court, can challenge or interrogate statements that have been made in the course of parliamentary proceedings.

The aim of this privilege is to ensure that parliamentarians are able to carry out their functions without fear of civil proceedings or criminal prosecution being brought against them.

This immunity has been subject to recent public consideration in the case of well-known public figures and the super injunction. In two recent examples, the businessman Sir Phillip Green and the footballer Ryan Giggs were named in parliament contrary to legal protections that they had both secured.

It should be further noted that there is no formal definition of what actually constitutes 'Proceedings in Parlyament', and it is in fact the courts who decide whether a particular activity does fall within the protections afforded by Article 9.

It is generally accepted that parliamentary proceedings include motions, debates, votes, parliamentary questions, work within committees, the work of officials of either House that arises out of proceedings of the House, and the work of the parliamentary standards commissioners.

THE RIGHT TO MANAGE AND CONTROL COMPOSITION AND PROCEDURES

As well as the protection offered by Article 9 of the Bill of Rights 1689, the concept of parliamentary privilege also extends to the protection of the right of each House to manage their own affairs and to have sole jurisdiction over their own proceedings.

This ensures that Parliament can decide what procedures to adopt, whether those procedures have been subject to a breach, and any consequences that may follow from a breach.

Recent examples of this process in action relate to the ability of Parliament to regulate the conduct of MPs with the House holding the right to suspend parliamentarians for misconduct. During 2022 and 2023, suspensions were placed upon Neale MacAskill, Paul Bristow, Margaret Ferrier, and Peter Bone for a range of infractions including disorderly conduct, breach of Covid lockdown rules, and bullying and sexual misconduct towards a staff member.

2.3.2 Executive Power and the Crown

The concept of executive power is often a challenge to adequately define. It can be stated to broadly include the power to manage public affairs and to have the power to implement the law itself.

Historically, the executive in the UK would have been solely attributable to one person, the monarch of the day. However, in more recent years, the power of the executive is a broader concept with power exercised by government ministers, the Prime Minister, and the Cabinet, as well as Scottish, Welsh, and Northern Irish ministers as well.

Additionally, there are a raft of public authorities who also exercise executive functions, and these include the Bank of England, the police, the Crown Prosecution Service, Her Majesty's Armed Forces, and the NHS.

In considering how executive power operates within the UK, we will primarily consider power through the centralised functions of government.

The starting point is that His Majesty's Government carries out the function of running the country and this is completed ostensibly on behalf of the Crown. In practical terms this means that government enforces the law and applies the law whilst the UK Parliament has the role of passing and enacting the law. It is then the role of the judiciary to interpret the law. It should also be noted that where secondary legislation is required, such as statutory instruments, that executive powers are granted to individual ministers.

Each of these roles involves the use of power on behalf of the Crown.

2.3.2.1 The Monarch and the Crown

It should be noted, rather confusingly, that the term the Crown is often used to mean two completely different things. Firstly, the term can be used as a means to describe the monarch of the day. At the same time, the term can also be used to describe the executive as a whole.

As noted previously, the monarch was the original all-powerful head of state in the UK. However, these powers have been reduced significantly, as discussed in Chapter 1, with the majority of Crown powers now exercised via the executive branch of the state, acting in the name of the Crown.

It should be noted that the Crown still retains a number of residual executive and legislative powers.

2.3.2.2 Central Government and Accountability

It is important at this point to note that the system of executive power is such that it creates a significant issue, if unchecked. As Lord Acton said:

Power tends to corrupt; absolute power corrupts absolutely.

The system therefore ensures that all are subject to the law, and this includes the government or executive. This is achieved through the mechanisms that exist to ensure executive accountability.

The three main mechanisms are as follows:

1) Parliament
   It is the responsibility of Parliament, and more specifically, the Members of Parliament, to ensure that the executive is held accountable. This is achieved via the legislative process (see 2.1.3.2), in which MPs are required to determine whether to support the policy agenda. It is also notable that MPs are there to represent the interests of their constituents and this can be directly, through the raising of issues within Parliament, or indirectly through their stance upon votes within Parliament. Should an MP ignore the will of constituents, then those very same constituents can decide to remove an MP either through disciplinary processes or as part of the electoral process.
2) Judicial
   Judicial scrutiny of the executive is a fundamental means of holding the executive accountable. Via the process of judicial review, the Administrative Court of the High Court can scrutinise the executive's policies, actions, and omissions. If the court finds that the executive has acted in a manner that is deemed illegal, irrational, a breach of natural justice, or the result of procedural impropriety, then the decision itself can be quashed by the court.
3) Electoral
   The electorate has the legal right to choose their parliamentary representative every five years.
   In addition, under the Recall of MPs Act 2015, a sitting MP can be removed from their seat in the House of Commons if one of three situations has occurred. These are:
   1) The MP has been convicted of an offence and receives a custodial sentence.
   2) The MP is suspended by the Committee for Standards for a period of more than 10 sitting days, or 14 days.
   3) The MP is convicted, under section 10 of the Parliamentary Standards Act 2009 – offence of providing false or misleading information for an allowance claim.

   Where one of the three conditions has been met, the Speakers of the House of Commons will notify the petition officer for the constituency who will open a recall petition. The recall petition will be successful if at least 10% of registered electors in that constituency sign the petition. A successful petition results in the MP's seat becoming vacant, after which a by-election is held.

2.3.2.3 *The Crown and Royal Prerogative*

Historically, the royal prerogative was the monarch's absolute power to do as they pleased. Over time, these powers have been limited with control passed to either the legislature or the judiciary.

The current position is that the royal prerogative is now a matter to be determined under the common law, whereby judges maintain the existence, extent, and limits of prerogative power.

The prerogative can be divided into three general areas.

1) Constitutional
   Under the royal prerogative, the Sovereign maintains a constitutional role in the appointment of a Prime Minister and in the granting of Royal Assent to legislation. The monarch also has a role in advising ministers.
2) Legal
   There still remains a range of legal prerogatives held by the Crown. These cover a variety of different positions from the Crown being deemed unable to do anything wrong under the law, unless specifically stated within the law, or via direct implication. The Crown is also entitled to a number of animals including whales, swans, and sturgeon.
3) Executive
   These powers include the ability to sign and ratify international conventions, deployment of HM Armed Forces, and powers of diplomacy. These powers are now typically the preserve of government ministers under constitutional convention.

It is important to note the hierarchy that exists in regards to the residual prerogative powers. As outlined in the case of *Attorney-General v De Keyser's Royal Hotel* [1920] AC 508, where a conflict exists between the prerogative power and statute, it is statute that the courts will utilise to reach a decision.

Similarly, should it be the will of Parliament, statute can be used to replace any aspect of residual prerogative power that may remain.

2.3.3 Judicial Power

Judicial power is the third element of the state and is characterised by two essential components. Firstly, that the judiciary must be independent from other branches of the state and, secondly, that independence must be aligned with security of tenure for judges.

The independence of the judiciary has not always been a facet of the UK constitutional structure. In fact, the development of judicial independence has been a piecemeal process. In fact, it was only in the Constitutional Reform Act 2005 that judicial independence was actually given a statutory footing. Under this act the House of Lords was removed as the highest court of the land and was replaced by the Supreme Court, a body wholly independent of Parliament.

Regarding security of tenure, it should be noted within this notion that there are degrees of security in place. So whilst judges of the Supreme Court and the Senior Courts of England and Wales enjoy a very high level of security of tenure, this reduces as one moves down the judicial pyramid.

The seat of judicial power is located within the role that the courts perform. The court's primary purpose is to adjudicate upon legal disputes between parties and to then render a verdict that upholds the concepts of the rule of law, equality, due process, and fairness.

Within this role, the courts are required to interpret the law with a view to determining the legal meaning of legislation passed by Parliament. Within this role sits great power that, through the common law approach, will then become binding upon future judgments.

2.3.3.1 The Role of the Courts and Tribunals

To understand how judicial power operates, it is important to understand the role that is played by the various courts that operate in England and Wales.

THE SUPREME COURT

Prior to October 2009, the highest court of appeal in the UK was the House of Lords. The Constitutional Reform Act 2005 replaced the House of Lords with a new Supreme Court.

The Supreme Court is the final court of appeal for all United Kingdom civil cases and criminal cases from England, Wales, and Northern Ireland.

The court also hears appeals on arguable points of law that are deemed to be of general public or constitutional importance.

THE JUDICIAL COMMITTEE OF THE PRIVY COUNCIL

The Judicial Committee of the Privy Council is the highest court of appeal for many commonwealth states (including Grenada, Jamaica, Tuvalu, and the Bahamas), as well as for United Kingdom overseas territories (including Bermuda, Gibraltar, Montserrat, and the Falkland Islands), Crown dependencies (Jersey, Guernsey, and the Isle of Man), and military sovereign base areas (such as Akrotiri and Dhekalia in Cyprus).

THE COURT OF APPEAL

The Court of Appeal is the highest court within the Senior Courts of England and Wales, dealing with appeals from other courts and tribunals.

The Court of Appeal is divided into two divisions, namely the Criminal Division and the Civil Division. Matters before the court are heard by the judges of the Court of Appeal, these are the Lord/Lady Chief Justice, the Master of the Rolls, the President of the King's Bench Division, the President of the Family Division, the Chancellor of the High Court, and the Lord and Lady Justices.

The Civil Division of the court hears appeals from all three divisions of the High Court of Justice and the specialist courts contained within, such as the Administrative Court. They also hear appeals from the county and family courts.

The Criminal Division hears appeals from the Crown Court.

THE HIGH COURT

The High Court of Justice in London, together with the Court of Appeal, comprises the Senior Courts of England and Wales. The High Court deals with high-value civil matters and other civil matters deemed as important cases. The High Court also holds a supervisory position over the majority of subordinate courts and tribunals.

The High Court consists of three divisions: the King's Bench, the Family, and the Chancery.

THE COUNTY COURT

The County Court deals with civil matters including debt recovery, compensation claims for personal injury, and property disputes. The court hears contested cases with typical values between £10,000 and £25,000 – although this can be increased with permission from a designated Civil Judge.

THE FAMILY COURT

As the name suggests, the Family Court is responsible for cases that involve disputes within families. These disputes are typically characterised as either private or public cases.

Private cases are disputes between parents and concern their children. These can involve matters of divorce, separation, child access, child residence, child education, and upbringing.

Public cases are family law cases that involve local authorities. These typically involve the removal of children from their parent's care due to risk of abuse or neglect.

THE CROWN COURT

The Crown Court is responsible for dealing with the most serious criminal cases, such as murder, violent assault, and rape. In the Crown Court, defendants will normally be tried by a jury who will seek to render a verdict of guilty or not guilty based upon the evidence placed before the court. The judge then has the role of deciding on the appropriate sentence, within the sentencing guidelines.

THE MAGISTRATES' COURT

It is important to note that all criminal cases actually start at the Magistrates' Court with the more serious offences being transferred to the Crown Court.

Cases that remain with the Magistrates' Court are known as summary offences and include matters of minor criminal damage, common assault, and most motoring offences. More serious offences such as burglary and drug offences can also be heard by the Magistrates' Court but this will depend on the facts of each given case.

There are no juries within the Magistrates' Court with cases heard either by a district judge or by two or three magistrates.

TRIBUNALS

There are many different areas of law where a matter can be brought before a tribunal rather than a court.

Tribunals themselves have a wide variety of administrative structures with some organised by His Majesty's Courts and Tribunals Service, whilst others may be administered through either local authorities or directly by government departments.

The tribunals administered by the Courts and Tribunal Service operate via a two-tier system – with the First-tier Tribunal providing the initial judgment of the case and with the Upper Tribunal being the first seat of appeal available.

Tribunals often sit on a panel basis with a tribunal judge joined by further panel members who may have expertise in the specific areas of the case. Like a court, they hear evidence from witnesses before reaching a verdict.

Tribunal decisions can include the imposing of fines, the award of compensation, the allowing or removal of benefit entitlement, or the ability to remain in the UK.

2.3.3.2 The Role of Ombudsmen

An ombudsman is a person appointed to look into complaints about companies and organisations. They are a free, independent, and impartial route to seek remedy when something has gone wrong.

In the UK there are a wide range of ombudsman schemes available, and these can largely be split into two groups – private sector and public sector.

Private sector ombudsman schemes operate when a complaint needs to be made about a commercial organisation who are affiliated with an ombudsman scheme.

Examples of private sector ombudsman schemes include the energy ombudsman (for complaints about gas and electricity suppliers), the communications ombudsman (for complaints against phone and internet providers), the motor ombudsman (for complaints against motor vehicle dealers, service and repair centres), and the financial ombudsman service (dealing with problems in regards to banks, insurance companies, pension providers, and mortgage and loan brokers.)

Public sector ombudsman schemes are available to deal with complaints regarding government departments, local authorities, and local service providers.

Examples include the Parliamentary and Health Ombudsman (for complaints about NHS service providers and community health services), the Local Government and Social Care Ombudsman (for complaints about councils and care service providers), the housing ombudsman (who assists tenants and leaseholders in disputes involving their landlord), and the Prisons and Probation Ombudsman (who carry out independent investigations into deaths and complaints relating to conduct whilst in custody).

2.3.3.3 Commissioners

The term commissioner is applied to a wide range of roles that include legal and administrative functions. Commissioners may:

- Act as the decision-maker within individual government departments.
- Hold a role in the regulation of standards within policy areas.
- Act in a judicial or quasi-judicial capacity.

Examples of relevant commissions include the Information Commissioner (which upholds information rights in the public interest), the Traffic Commissioner (who licences and regulates HGV and PCV licences), Police and Crime Commissioners (a role that involves the promotion of people's views within a constabulary area and ensuring that the police force are held accountable), and the Children's Commissioner (who promotes and protects the rights of children).

Chapter 2 Revision Points

This chapter has introduced the main seats of power that exist within the UK constitution, with a view to assisting the reader to understand how everything from parliament is organised through to how legislation becomes law and how that law is then subject to interpretation by the judiciary.

We have observed that the structures are connected in an evolving and ongoing manner that ensures that control is managed and that effective balance exists to meet the needs of the population as a whole.

Multiple Choice Questions

Question 1

Upon retiring from the House of Commons, Mrs Smith is made a life peer.

Which of the following best describes the part Mrs Smith can play in the legislative process as a peer in the House of Lords?

A. As a life peer, Mrs Smith will have a purely ceremonial role and will have no say in legislation.
B. As a life peer, Mrs Smith can vote against proposed legislation to prevent the bill from becoming law.
C. Mrs Smith will be able to debate legislative content but only if the proposed bill relates to major issues of public interest.
D. Life peers are only able to approve bills that have already been debated and approved by the House of Commons.
E. As a life peer, Mrs Smith can scrutinise legislation and propose amendments to bills.

Question 2

Immediately prior to the opening of Parliament, the King decides to add a new law, on environmental control, into his speech.

Doe the UK constitution have any means to prevent the King from adding the new law?

A. Yes, this can be prevented as it would be a breach of an Act of Parliament.
B. Yes, this can be prevented as it would breach a constitutional convention.
C. Yes, this can be prevented as it would not be possible under the common law.
D. No, there is nothing written in the constitution that would prevent the King from changing his speech.
E. No, as the King has sovereign powers, he is able to amend the speech.

Question 3

Following civil disturbances across the UK, the Home Secretary seeks to equip all police officers with a new form of plastic bullet using powers available under the minister's executive powers via royal prerogative. It is confirmed by the leader of the opposition that this step is prohibited under the recent Criminal Justice Act, which does not permit the use of the suggested plastic bullet on UK streets.

Can the Home Secretary use the royal prerogative and issue the plastic bullets to the police?

A. Yes, as maintaining the King's Peace is a duty of the Home Secretary and so the royal prerogative can be used in this fashion.
B. Yes, it is within the minister's powers under the royal prerogative, and this is supported by the existing statutory framework.
C. No, the royal prerogative cannot be used in this fashion as the matter has been covered within the statute.
D. No, the royal prerogative cannot be used as described as court approval has not been granted.
E. No, the royal prerogative cannot be used as described as the Home Secretary would firstly need the approval of the full Cabinet.

PART 3

Supremacy, the Rule of Law, and the Separation of Powers

3 Supremacy, the Rule of Law, and the Separation of Powers

3.1 SQE1 Syllabus

The SQE1 syllabus requires that an individual has an awareness of a wide range of constitutional and administrative topics. These include an understanding of the concept of parliamentary sovereignty (or supremacy), the rule of law, and the separation of powers between the three branches of the state. In this chapter, we will be looking to build upon the previous two chapters to enable the reader to contextualise this area of law.

3.2 Chapter Overview

Within this chapter we will evaluate parliamentary supremacy through consideration of the principle, the regulation of the concept, and the restrictions that ensure that Parliament does not become too powerful. This will be considered in the context of systems of precedence from external sources such as the EU.

The chapter will also consider the theoretical concept of the rule of law before considering how this is interpreted via the judiciary. Finally, we will consider the separation of powers and again the role that the judiciary plays in interpreting the effect of separation across the branches of the state.

3.3 Parliamentary Supremacy

The doctrine of parliamentary supremacy is based on the notion of a sovereign parliament that holds power. The principle was first conceived by John Locke, a 17th-century political philosopher, who put forward the view that the electorate transfer their sovereignty to their parliamentary representative through the act of representation. Once the sovereignty of the people has been transferred, Parliament then becomes the supreme lawmaking authority, accountable only to the electorate.

This view followed a period of great upheaval in the history of the nation. In the 1640s, the country had been though the English Civil War, and this was followed by the trial and execution of Charles I.

DOI: 10.4324/9781032642024-7

In the decades that followed, William of Orange landed his army in England and in 1689 a meeting was summoned of peers and commoners. The meeting declared itself to be the Parliament of England and took a vital step forward, in constitutional terms, by passing the Bill of Rights.

The Bill of Rights 1689 reset the balance of power between the monarch and Parliament in favour of Parliament.

3.3.1 Principle of Supremacy

The writer A.V. Dicey, in his text *An Introduction to the Study of the Law of the Constitution*, stated:

> The principle of parliamentary sovereignty means neither more nor less than this: namely, that Parliament . . . has, under the English constitution, the right to make or unmake any law whatever; and, further, that no person or body is recognised by the law . . . as having a right to override or set aside the legislation of Parliament.

Dicey's definition can be broken down into three main parts:

1) Parliament has the power to make or unmake any law, without limitation. This clearly gives Parliament great powers in shaping the legal, political, and social landscape of the country.
2) Parliament cannot be bound by a previous Parliament nor can Parliament bind a future Parliament.
3) Supremacy requires that the courts do not strike down the laws made by Parliament. While courts can interpret the law and determine the meaning, they cannot set aside or specifically overrule laws that have been made by Parliament.

This last point is important to consider in further detail via consideration of the 'enrolled act' rule.

Enrolled Act Rule

The enrolled act rule originates with the case of *The King v Arundel* [1616] EWHC J11 (Ch) and is based on the concept that any act that has passed through the required stages of Parliament, prior to then receiving Royal Assent, has been granted 'the effective legal act of enactment'. It is at that point the act is 'a regal Act, and no official might dispute the King's word'.

The rule was restated by Lord Campbell in the case of *Edinburgh & Dalkeith Railway Co v Wauchope* (1842) 8 Cl & F 710. In that case, it was claimed that the enactment of a private Act of Parliament had been defective due to a failure to provide adequate notice. The House of Lords rejected the notion that the act was invalid, with Lord Campbell stating:

> All that a court of justice can do is to look to the Parliamentary Roll: if from that it should appear that a bill has passed both Houses and received Royal Assent, no court of justice can enquire into the mode in which it was introduced into Parliament, what was done previously to it being introduced . . . or what passed . . . during its progress . . . through Parliament.

In the case of *Pickin v British Railways Board* [1974] AC 765, the House of Lords confirmed that there existed no power for them to disregard an Act of Parliament or for the courts to examine the proceedings of Parliament in passing the act. Lord Morris stated:

> It must surely be for Parliament to lay down the procedures which are to be followed before a Bill can become an Act. It must be for Parliament to decide whether its decreed procedures have been followed.

As A.V. Dicey's definition confirms, there are no limits placed upon the legislative powers of Parliament, and this can be demonstrated through a series of examples and cases.

1) Statute may remove or restrict the operation of the royal prerogative.
   Examples include the Crown Proceedings Act 1947, the Fixed Term Parliaments Act 2011, and the European Union (Notification of Withdrawal) Act 2017.
2) Statute will take precedence over constitutional conventions.
   An example of this is found in the passing of the Southern Rhodesia Act 1965 where Lord Reid rejected the argument that parliamentary sovereignty could be limited by constitutional conventions.
3) Statute may alter the constitution.
   There are a number of examples that demonstrate the ability of legislation to alter the very constitution of the country; these include the Acts of Union 1706–1707, the Parliament Acts 1911 and 1949, and the Human Rights Act 1998.
4) Statute can override provisions of international law.
   In the case of Cheney v Conn [1968] 1 All ER 779, Judge Ungoed-Thomas, sitting in the Chancery Division of the High Court, stated:
   > If the purpose for which a statute may be used is an invalid purpose, then such remedy as there may be must be directed to dealing with that purpose and not to invalidating the statute itself. What the statute itself enacts cannot be unlawful, because what the statute says and provides is itself the law, and the highest form of law that is known to this country. It is the law which prevails over every other form of law, and it is not for the court to say that a parliamentary enactment, the highest law in this country, is illegal.
5) Statute can also operate retrospectively.
   The main authority on this point is the War Damage Act 1965, which was enacted in response to the decision in Burmah Oil Co v Lord Advocate [1965] AC 75.

The case concerned the actions of the British Armed Forces during the Second World War. As part of the Japanese invasion of Burma in 1942, the British had taken the step of destroying the oil fields that were owned and operated by the Burmah Oil Company to prevent the precious resource falling into the hands of the Japanese. The majority decision of the House of Lords was that this act of destruction was the equivalent of requisitioning the property of Burmah Oil and was therefore compensable.

However, the War Damage Act was enacted with provisions that had retrospective effect and this therefore removed the right of the claimant to compensation.

As can be seen, in these examples, the power of parliamentary supremacy is vast and far reaching; it is therefore important to consider the systems that exist to restrict this power.

3.3.2 Restrictions of Supremacy

There exists a range of both domestic and external controls that seek to limit the supremacy of Parliament. We will look at each in turn.

Domestic Limitations

There exists a range of rules, doctrines, and statutes that domestically have the effect of restricting the power of parliamentary supremacy.

The Acts of Union

The formation of the United Kingdom was commenced by the creation of the Treaty of Union. The treaty detailed how the Parliaments of England and Scotland were willing to vest their powers and authority into a new Great British Parliament.

The treaty was given legal effect by the Acts of Union 1706–1707 which also made explicit provision for the preservation of the Church of Scotland and also the Scottish legal system.

It is argued that the combination of these provisions within the act are binding upon future Parliaments and thereby restrict the doctrine of parliamentary supremacy.

The matter was subject to obiter comment in the case of *MacCormick v Lord Advocate* 1953 (Scot) SC 396. In this case (perhaps showing that the law will truly allow people to bring an action about anything) the rector of the University of Glasgow, John MacCormick, and Ian Hamilton, a Scottish Nationalist, contested the right of Queen Elizabeth II to style herself as Elizabeth II in Scotland. It was claimed by the two gentleman that this was a breach of the Act of Union 1707, as there had been no previous Queen Elizabeth of Scotland (Elizabeth I was the Queen of England only).

The case was, perhaps unsurprisingly, unsuccessful, but the obiter comments of Lord President Lord Cooper, Lord Carmont, and Lord Russell were of interest. Lord President Lord Cooper stated, 'the principle of unlimited sovereignty of Parliament is a distinctively English principle and has no counterpart in Scottish constitutional law'.

The Lord Advocate, who was representing the Crown in the case, conceded this point by admitting that the United Kingdom Parliament 'could not repeal or alter fundamental and essential conditions' of the Act of Union.

Devolution

In May 1997, the Labour government of Tony Blair was elected on a manifesto of policies that included the creation of devolved institutions in Scotland, Wales, and Northern Ireland.

Later that same year a referendum was held and the resounding yes vote led to the creation of the Scottish Parliament. Similar outcomes were also achieved in Wales and in Northern Ireland.

The process of devolution to the nations of the United Kingdom established a set of devolved legislative powers. These allow the national assemblies to create laws within set policy areas, such as health, education, and legal affairs, without requiring any agreement from the UK Parliament.

This position ensures that while Westminster retains ultimate authority, it is the policy decisions of the devolved bodies to which the UK Parliament defers.

Whilst the devolved governments may legislate only to the extent that the UK Parliament allows them to do so, this is still a clear restriction upon the doctrine.

In addition, whilst the UK Parliament can look to pass legislation for the devolved nations, the Sewel Convention confirms that the UK Parliament 'will not normally legislate with regard to devolved matters without the consent' of the devolved legislature.

It is noted following the referendum on leaving the European Union that there is some evidence of the UK Parliament being willing to override the subordinate jurisdiction. Sections of both the European Union (Withdrawal Act) 2018 and the European Union (Withdrawal Agreement) Act 2020 related to policy matters that were devolved, although it should be added that the matter of international relations is an activity reserved to the UK Parliament.

When the Scottish Parliament refused to consent to the bills, the UK Parliament simply continued the legislative process leading to the enacting of the legislation.

Implied Repeal

The implied repeal doctrine confirms that a later Act of Parliament repeals an earlier act, without there being any specific requirement for the later act to mention the predecessor.

This is a powerful tool within the armoury of parliamentary sovereignty. However, the case of *Thoburn v Sunderland City Council* [2002] EWHC 195 (Admin) calls into question the extent of this power.

In the case, Lord Justice Laws suggested that there existed two different types of statute and that the two should be considered separately of each other. The first type would be considered to be 'ordinary' statutes, and these would be subject to all notions of implied repeal. However, he proposed that a second type of statute – the 'constitutional' statutes – should not be subject to implied intention.

In cases where the courts were to change path from prior legislation, constitutional statutes would require actual intention to be demonstrated by Parliament.

This, of course, raised the question of what a constitutional statute is, and a test was proposed involving two possible limbs:

1) The statute would be considered constitutional if it impacted upon the legal relationship between the state and the citizen in a general manner; or
2) The statute would be constitutional in nature if it sought to change the scope of a fundamental constitutional right.

Lord Justice Laws stated:

> We should recognise a hierarchy of Acts of Parliament: as it were 'ordinary' statutes and 'constitutional' statutes . . . Examples are the Magna Carta, the bill of Rights 1689 . . . the Human Rights Act 1998 . . . [and] . . . the European Communities Act . . . Ordinary statutes may be impliedly repealed. Constitutional statutes may not.

The views expressed in the Thoburn case have been supported in subsequent decisions of the Supreme Court.

In *H v Lord Advocate* [2012] UKSC 24 Lord Hope explored, in obiter comment, how apparent contradictions between the Extradition Act 2003 and the Scotland Act 1998 should be approached. He said:

> It would perhaps have been open to Parliament to override the [relevant] provisions of [the Scotland Act] . . . But in my opinion only an express provision to that effect could be held to lead to such a result. This is because of the fundamental constitutional nature of the settlement that was achieved by the Scotland Act.

Clearly, the operation of the doctrine of implied repeal would have simply ensured that the Extradition Act would have overridden the Scotland Act but this was not the case.

Similarly, in the case of *R (HS2 Action Alliance Ltd) v Secretary of State for Transport* [2014] UKSC 3, the judgment at paragraph 207 states:

> The United Kingdom has no written constitution, but we have a number of constitutional instruments. They include Magna Carta, the Petition of Right 1628, the Bill of Rights and (in Scotland) the Claim of Rights Act 1689, the Act of Settlement 1701 and the Act of Union 1707. The European Communities Act 1972, the Human Rights Act 1998 and the Constitutional Reform Act 2005 may now be added to this list. The common law itself also recognises certain principles as fundamental to the rule of law. It is, putting the point at its lowest, certainly arguable (and it is for United Kingdom law and courts to determine) that there may be fundamental principles, whether contained in other constitutional instruments or recognised at common law, of which Parliament when it enacted the European Communities Act 1972 did not either contemplate or authorise the abrogation.

The judgment confirms that there exists a number of acts to which courts will not apply the concept of implied repeal, without specific authority from Parliament.

Manner and Form

A further consideration is termed as the manner and form debate. This states that whilst Parliament cannot bind its successors through legislation, it may be possible for an earlier Parliament to bind a future Parliament regarding the procedure which Parliament requires in the enactment of legislation.

There is substantial academic theory postulating the case for and the case against this approach, which goes beyond the scope of this text.

However, the case of *R (Jackson) v Attorney General* [2005] UKHL 56 suggested that whilst there may be limits to parliamentary supremacy in this area, the whole area is unclear.

This lack of clarity was perhaps best encapsulated by the judgments of Lord Steyn and Lord Hope.

With Lord Steyn stating:

> Parliament could for specific purposes provide for a two-thirds majority in the House of Commons and the House of Lords. This would involve a redefinition of Parliament for a specific purpose. Such redefinition could not be disregarded.

Whilst Lord Hope proffered:

> it is a fundamental aspect of the rule of sovereignty that no Parliament can bind its successors. There are no means whereby . . . it can entrench an Act of Parliament.

"Henry VIII" Clauses

Henry VIII clauses are clauses added into bills that enable the relevant minister to either amend or repeal aspects within Acts of Parliament through the use of secondary legislation. By using secondary legislation, the minister can avoid some aspects of parliamentary scrutiny of the legislative amendment.

Again, this has a significant role in potentially reducing the power of parliamentary supremacy, as it would be a minister, rather than Parliament, who is making or changing the law.

Due to this, the Lords Delegated Powers and Regulatory Reform Committee inspects any proposed bill with a view to indicating if such a clause is present and the justification, if any, for it being included.

The Rule of Law

Whilst we will consider the rule of law in detail within the next section, it is important to note that this may also be a restricting factor upon parliamentary supremacy.

In the case of *Moohan v Lord Advocate* [2014] UKSC 67, Lord Hodge suggested:

> I do not exclude the possibility that in the very unlikely event that a parliamentary majority abusively sought to entrench its power by a curtailment of the franchise or similar device, the common law, informed by principles of democracy and the rule of law and international norms, would be able to declare such legislation unlawful.

Although he continued to state that this would be a matter for debate, his view did echo Lord Steyn's view in *R (Jackson) v Attorney General* [2005] UKHL 56, that judges could qualify the principle of parliamentary sovereignty as it was a 'construct of the common law'.

External Limitations

The reach of parliamentary supremacy is also constrained by external factors including the doctrine of supremacy of European Union Law, the direct effect principle, the indirect effect principle, and the European Convention on Human Rights.

3.4 The Rule of Law

The rule of law is a fundamental aspect of the British constitution. At its core is the principle going back to Magna Carta in 1215, that not even the monarch is above the law.

At its heart the rule of law is present to prevent abuse of state power, is a universal constant in the application of the law to all, and also ensures that legal rights and freedoms are fulfilled.

Whilst there is no universally agreed definition of the rule of law, it contains a series of core concepts including legality, equality, the protection of fundamental rights, an independent judiciary, access to justice, and legal certainty.

A.V. Dicey, in *An Introduction to the Study of the Law of the Constitution* (1885), defined the rule of law through three parameters:

1) No man is punishable or can be lawfully made to suffer in body or goods except for a distinct breach of the law established in the ordinary legal manner before the ordinary courts of the land. . . . It means . . . the absolute supremacy . . . of regular law as opposed to the influence of arbitrary power.
2) no man is above the law . . . every man and woman, whatever be his rank or condition, is subject to the ordinary law of the realm and amenable to the jurisdiction of the ordinary tribunals.
3) the general principles of the constitution are with us as a result of judicial decisions . . . in particular cases brought before the courts.

Whilst Dicey's definition was written at a time before many areas of development within the Administrative Law were even contemplated, it does provide a back-drop by which to consider the rule of law today.

And it is important to note how important the rule of law remains to this day.

The rule of law prevents abuse of state power, it ensures that the law is applicable and is followed by all, and it ensures that legal rights are available to us all. It is also an important backdrop to many other fundamental aspects of the democratic process, such as the protected right to have free and fair elections, and also ensures that the law is bound to give legal effect to the laws that have been passed within the democratically elected parliament.

Looking at the rule of law from a wider perspective, it can also be observed that the doctrine also supports the very fabric of society via the legal process that flows from the principle. In addition, it is clear that even areas such as economic growth and stability within the economy can be traced back to the rule of law through the upholding of property rights, the illegality of corrupt practices, and the maintenance of commercial contracts that underpin national and international trade.

With the influence of the rule of law clearly vital to the operation of our democracy, it has been subject to ongoing interpretation.

3.4.1 Theories of the Rule of Law

A.V. Dicey

As we have observed, the starting point to considering the rule of law has to be Albert Venn Dicey. Dicey was a 19th-century English legal theorist who highlighted many aspects of the rule of law that are still considered important today. These include the distrust of arbitrary power and the fundamental principle of equality before the law.

However, Dicey's view has been long criticised as being too England-centric, with the wording almost seeming to suggest that England was the only country in the world that is governed by a rule of law approach. It is also noted that Dicey's view was not able to see how administrative law would develop, particularly regarding, for example, the exercise of powers by public officials and public bodies.

Lord Bingham

Lord Tom Bingham held a range of high legal offices including Lord Chief Justice of England and Wales and Master of the Rolls, and he was also a Senior Law Lord. In addition to his judicial career, he was a passionate speaker on the rule of law and he published a book on the doctrine in 2010.

In the book, Lord Bingham laid out eight principles that underpin the rule of law. These are:

1) The law must be accessible and, so far as possible, intelligible, clear, and predictable;
2) Questions of legal right and liability should ordinarily be resolved by application of the law, and not the exercise of discretion;
3) The laws of the land should apply equally to all, save to the extent that objective differences justify differentiation;
4) Legal protection of such human rights as, within that society, are seen as fundamental;
5) Means must be provided for resolving, without prohibitive cost or inordinate delay, bona fide civil disputes which the parties themselves are unable to resolve;
6) Ministers and public officers at all levels must exercise the powers conferred on them reasonably, in good faith, for the purpose for which the powers were conferred, and without exceeding the limits of such powers;

7) The adjudicative procedures provided by the state should be fair; and
8) Compliance by the state with its obligations in international law.

It is clear that whilst Lord Bingham's definition has clear similarities to that of A.V. Dicey, for example, in terms of certainty of laws and the abiding concept of equality before the law, it is notable that Bingham's approach is often considered to be more helpful. This is particularly true when we look to the rule of law as an international concept, with Bingham's view supporting the position that any definition of the rule of law does not require anything specifically English to be included. Instead the principles should be principles that countries around the world could aspire to.

That is not to say that Lord Bingham's eight factors have not come in for criticism. The broad nature of the definition has been considered to be too wide by many who question whether human rights and compliance with international law are required. It is also said that the use of so many factors reads more like a shopping list of ideal characteristics rather than an explanation of the rule of law.

Professor Martin Krygier

Professor Krygier is an Australian legal theorist and former member of the Rule of Law Institute. In his interpretation of the doctrine, there are clear differences from many of the other approaches that have been taken. Krygier puts forward that the rule of law is 'to temper or moderate the exercise of power, in order to avoid its arbitrary use'.

He then proceeds to turn the exercise of definition on its head somewhat by arguing that instead of lists of principles, we should simply identify what the rule of law seeks to achieve and then we should proceed to identify the institutions and mechanisms that will allow for that purpose to be achieved. In essence the rule of law is simply a construct comprised of those institutions and mechanisms that advance the specified purpose of a particular society at a specified point in time.

Whilst it is noted that this approach allows for an evolving rule of law, in tune with the requirements of a country at a given period in its own development, it can be observed that this can be too wide an approach to take with no core principle holding the doctrine together.

Professor Joseph Raz

Professor Raz was a legal, moral, and political philosopher who was an advocate of the legal positivism school. He was also the winner of the Tang Prize in Rule of Law in 2018.

In his text *The Authority of Law*, Raz argued that the main function of the rule of law is to ensure that 'the law should conform to standards designed to enable it effectively to guide action'.

In Raz's view, the rule of law only provides a general framework in which the laws of a country should operate. In his view the law should:

- Be accessible to the wider public.
- Be without retrospective effect.
- Be made using appropriate procedure.
- Be stable in nature and not therefore subject to arbitrary or frequent change.
- Be a basis for the open and fair administration or justice.
- Be administered via an independent judiciary.

It can be observed that the views of Raz were more in line with those of A.V. Dicey but again were subject to criticism, with one view stating that an authoritarian dictatorship could comply with the provisions and therefore claim to operate within the rule of law!

3.4.2 Judicial Interpretation of the Rule of Law

As with all aspects of the law, it would not be appropriate to conclude our analysis of the rule of law without some consideration of how the various aspects considered previously have been reflected within judicial decisions.

The Rule of Law Concept

There are a number of examples from within recent judicial precedent that make mention of the rule of law as a general concept.

The case of *R (Jackson) v Attorney General* [2005] UKHL 56 provides an example.

The case concerned the passing of the Hunting Act 2004, an act that prohibited the practice of fox hunting. The initial bill for this illustrated much about the respective powers of the Commons and the Lords, with the Commons supporting the bill at each stage, whilst the Lords continually opposed the proposed legislation.

Due to this the Parliament Act 1949 was used as a means to bypass the Lords opposition and the bill subsequently proceeded and was granted Royal Assent.

The case focussed on whether the parliamentary process employed was valid, with the argument being that the Parliament Act 1949 could not be used in this case as the bill would affect fundamental constitutional changes.

Lord Hope, at paragraph 107 of the judgment, states:

> The rule of law enforced by the courts is the ultimate controlling factor on which our constitution is based. The fact that your Lordships have been willing to hear this appeal and to give judgment upon it is another indication that the courts have a part to play in defining the limits of Parliament's legislative sovereignty.

In addition, the courts have also shown a willingness to use the doctrine as a means to justify the judgments handed down across a wide range of cases. We shall consider a few such examples below.

A AND OTHERS V SECRETARY OF STATE FOR THE HOME DEPARTMENT [2005] 2 AC 68

The case related to the detention of foreign prisoners at HMP Belmarsh. The prisoners in question were held subject to section 23 of the Anti-terrorism, Crime and Security Act 2001 which permitted indefinite detention. This was challenged in terms of compatibility with the European Convention of Human Rights.

In the case the House of Lords held that the provisions under which the prisoners were detained were incompatible with Article 5 (right to liberty and security) and Article 14 (protection from discrimination) of the European Convention of Human Rights. The judgment was founded on the grounds of nationality, as whilst the 2001 act would permit foreign prisoners to be detained, the same provisions could not be applied to domestic terrorists.

In terms of the rule of law, the case is significant due to the comment of Lord Nicholls, who stated, 'indefinite imprisonment without charge or trial is anathema in any country which observes the rule of law . . . Wholly exceptional circumstances must exist before this extreme step can be justified'.

R (ANDERSON) V SECRETARY OF STATE FOR THE HOME DEPARTMENT [2002] UKHL 46; [2002] 4 ALL ER 1089

In this case Anderson had received mandatory life sentences after being convicted of the murder of a 60-year-old man in 1986 and a year later a 35-year-old man. The murders had been committed and the victim's property had been stolen. Under section 29 of the Crime (Sentences) Act 1997, the Home Secretary had the discretionary power to change the tariff associated with the sentence. The tariff being the minimum term that the prisoner must serve before they can be considered for release.

In the case at hand, the trial judge and the Lord Chief Justice had recommended that a minimum term of 15 years be served for both murders. However, the Home Secretary, exercising his discretion under section 29, set the tariff at a minimum of 20 years.

Anderson sought a judicial review of the decision on the basis that section 29 was incompatible with Article 6(1) of the European Convention of Human Rights (right to a fair trial by an independent and impartial tribunal), as the Home Secretary was not a tribunal within the meaning of Article 6(1).

The House of Lords allowed the appeal, declaring that section 29 was incompatible with Article 6(1).

Within his speech Lord Steyn stated:

> the proposition that a decision to punish an offender by ordering him to serve a period of imprisonment may only be made by a court of law . . . is a principal feature of the rule of law on which our unwritten constitution is based.

R (UNISON) V LORD CHANCELLOR [2017] UKSC 51

This is an employment and constitutional case regarding the fees that were required to be paid to bring a claim before the employment tribunal. The UK government, via the Employment Appeal Tribunal Fees Order 2013 (SI 2013/83), had introduced fees of around £1200 to bring a typical case to an employment tribunal.

The power to introduce the measure had been exercised under section 42(1) of the Tribunals, Courts and Enforcement Act 2007. The trade union UNISON brought the case claiming that the order was *ultra vires* (an act without the required legal authority). In their case it was stated, amongst other considerations, that the fees restricted access to justice.

The Supreme Court unanimously found in favour of the trade union.

In his judgment Lord Reed sought to explore the link between access to justice and the rule of law. His judgment had the effect of demonstrating a significant expansion of the rule of law into a doctrine that operates to regulate the content of public policy.

Sir Stephen Laws, writing for Policy Exchange, stated:

> The incontrovertible and sound principle that the executive must comply with the law transforms itself, in the reasoning of the judgment, into the idea that there are at least some areas of policy (the financial management of the justice system, it seems, is one) that are to be subjected to a judicial 'success test' under which the judiciary is able, with the benefit of hindsight, to second-guess and overturn political policy decisions by reference not to how they were made or implemented, but rather by reference to what, it turns out, has been their effect in practice.

M V HOME OFFICE [1993] UKHL 5

M was a citizen of Zaire (now the Democratic Republic of Congo). M had arrived in the UK and made an application for asylum. However, despite applying on multiple occasions, M was rejected each time, and he was informed that he was to be deported back to his country of birth. M made a further application to the High Court for a judicial review of the refusal to grant asylum. The judge requested that the deportation should be delayed with a view to allowing appropriate consideration of the case. However, at that point M was already on a flight from London to Paris, en route to Zaire.

Upon learning of the ongoing deportation, the judge took the step of ordering M's return. However, the Home Secretary, convinced that the asylum claim had been correctly rejected, cancelled the return arrangements. It was his view that the judge did not have the legal power to make an interim order against a minister of the Crown.

The case progressed to the House of Lords who held that the Home Secretary had acted in contempt of court and had to now take steps to return M to the UK.

Lord Templeman was critical of the Home Secretary's decision as he stated

> the argument that there is no power to enforce the law by injunction or contempt proceedings against a minister in his official capacity . . . [would] establish the proposition that the executive obey the law as a matter of grace and not as a matter of necessity, a proposition which would reverse the result of the Civil War.

In regard to the rule of law, Lord Woolf stated, 'the object of the exercise is not so much to punish an individual as to vindicate the rule of law by a finding of contempt'.

The judgment demonstrates the notion of equality before the law and the rule of law as central with no special privilege available to even those within ministerial positions.

3.5 The Separation of Powers

Closely aligned with the operational requirements of the rule of law is the concept of the separation of powers.

The concept requires that the principal institutions of state, namely the executive, the legislature, and the judiciary, should be clearly divided to ensure that liberties are protected and that no one institution can rule without balances placed upon their power.

The doctrine confirms that:

- The legislature makes the law.
- The executive implements the law.
- The judiciary resolves disputes about the law.

In the UK, the legislature comprises Parliament which itself comprises the Crown, the House of Commons, and the House of Lords. The executive comprises the Crown and the government led by the Prime Minister and Cabinet ministers. The judiciary comprises the judges of courts of law, those who hold office within the tribunal system, and lay magistrates who sit in the Magistrates' Court structure.

3.5.1 Purpose and History

Baron Montesquieu, in writing *The Spirit of the Law* (c1748), proclaimed:

> When the legislative and executive powers are united in the same person, or in the same body of magistrates, there can be no liberty . . . there is no liberty if the powers of judging is not separated from the legislative and executive . . . there would be an end to everything, if the same man or the same body . . . were to exercise those three powers.

Hilaire Barnett, author of *Constitutional and Administrative Law* (Routledge, 2019), states:

> The essence of the doctrine is that there should be, ideally, a clear demarcation of personnel and functions between the legislature, executive and judiciary in order that none should have excessive power, and that there should be in place a system of checks and balances between institutions.

Therefore, if the doctrine is strictly applied, none of the three branches of the state may exercise the power that is bestowed upon another. It is also the case that no individual should be a member of any two of the branches simultaneously.

If such an overlap existed, it is viewed that this would be too much power concentrated in one place, and this could lead to a failure of balance within the system.

As with many aspects of the constitutional arrangements that exist in the UK, there is no formal separation of powers. This is due to the unwritten, uncodified, and often ad hoc basis upon which the UK constitution is founded. In essence, there is no formal system of controls in place to ensure the ongoing maintenance of the separation of powers. The whole system is built upon informality and the established structures.

It is important to understand how the informal process and structures work to maintain order.

The Executive and the Legislature

The first area to consider is the relationship that exists between the executive (the government) and the legislature (Parliament). This area provides an interesting insight into how the processes and structures in the UK operate.

On the one hand, there already seems to be an issue present. Namely that the executive is made up of the ministers of state. However, those ministers, by convention, are drawn from the House of Commons or the House of Lords – clearly making the same people both members of the executive and members of the legislature simultaneously.

This is clearly an uneasy starting point in seeking to address how powers are separated.

However, there are some elements of statutory control present as well, with section 2 of the House of Commons Disqualification Act 1975 confirming that the maximum number of government ministers who may sit in the Commons is limited to 95. The idea behind the limit is that whilst 95 members of Parliament may hold roles within the executive, this would clearly be balanced by the 555 MPs who held just a role within the legislature.

In practice, though, this is a challenging argument to make as commentators have written about how the government effectively controls Parliament, with Lord Hailsham going so far as describing the UK system as an 'elective dictatorship'.

The former Lord Chancellor stated that although the electorate have the chance to select the party that they wish to govern the nation on a cyclical basis, once that decision is made the government of the day has effective control over the entire legislative programme. The only consideration that any government who holds a parliamentary majority must consider is that they will at some point have to submit themselves again to the electorate at the next general election. In the intervening period Parliament, rather than acting as an effective legislature, actually largely rubber stamps the legislation put forward by government.

That is not to say that Parliament does not exert control upon the government. Through a range of methods, it is possible for the legislature to perform some role in fettering the powers of the executive through:

- Debates

A debate in either the House of Commons or the House of Lords is a formal discussion that explores a specific proposal. Representatives of the relevant house take turns to speak. The debate process has many aspects that allow scrutiny of the will of the executive:

- Standing orders are the written rules which regulate the conduct of proceedings within each House. Within the rules it is permitted for an emergency debate to be called. An emergency debate is a debate that is called at short notice regarding a subject that is classified as a 'specific and important matter that should have urgent consideration'. The process of calling an emergency debate starts when an MP applies to the Speaker under Standing Order number 24. The Speaker will grant the debate, if it is considered that the topic is such that it is considered of national importance. If granted, the emergency debate takes place within 24 hours.

Similarly, within the standing orders, parliamentary time can be allocated for debates that are called by the official opposition.

As mentioned at 2.3.1.2, at the second reading stage, all government bills are debated by the House of Commons and then again at the second reading stage within the House of Lords.

- Through constitutional convention, it is a regular feature of parliamentary business that MPs are given the opportunity to ask questions to government ministers. Perhaps the most famous example of this is the process of Questions to the Prime Minister, often known as Prime Minister's Question Time or just PMQs. Every Wednesday at noon, MPs are able to ask questions of the Prime Minister for a 30-minute period held each week during the parliamentary session. The process of PMQs is largely fixed, with the leader of the official opposition able to ask up to six questions of the PM and the leader of the next largest party able to ask two questions. The remaining questions will be asked by backbench MPs who are selected via a ballot, or via the supplemental question approach where they stand and wait to be selected by the Speaker of the House.
- The House of Commons appoints general committees to consider proposed legislation. All government bills will be subject to line-by-line scrutiny within the committee stage and from here amendments to the bill can be made.
- In addition to general committees, select committees are set up to investigate and scrutinise specific issues in detail. The membership of select committees mirrors the configuration of Parliament, with only backbench MPs able to take up a role.
- Whilst a rare event, it should be noted that governments do suffer defeats on the House of Commons. This would be the clearest example of how the legislature constrains the executive.

Parliament and the Royal Prerogative

The very nature of how the royal prerogative operates as a power of the executive is such that it would often be seen as a challenge to the notion of effective control within the separation of powers doctrine.

It is clear that the use of the royal prerogative grants the executive considerable powers in matters of national security and armed forces deployment without any requirement for scrutiny by Parliament. In addition to the lack of any requirement for scrutiny by the legislature, there is also no requirement for the judiciary to question actions taken in this area as they are considered to be non-justiciable in nature.

Despite this, there is a growing sense that Parliament is becoming a more important factor in restraining the powers available to the executive under the royal prerogative. In recent conflicts in Iraq and Syria, the government has taken the step of seeking parliamentary approval before deploying the armed forces into the conflict zones. At present though this is yet to become a formal convention, as evidenced by the actions taken in Libya and in Mali without Parliament being consulted.

Chapter 3 Revision Points

This chapter has introduced the reader to three overarching concepts that underpin much of the constitutional arrangements of the UK. We have reviewed the concepts of parliamentary sovereignty, the rule of law, and the separation of powers with a view to ensuring understanding of how these doctrines underpin the core institutions of the state and how they interrelate.

We have observed that the structures are connected in an evolving and ongoing manner that ensures that control is managed and that effective balance exists.

Multiple Choice Questions

Question 1

A solicitor is asked to advise a client regarding a possible application for judicial review, against the decision to deny the client asylum in the UK. The client asks you about the term 'the rule of law' and its meaning.

Which of the following states the best response?

A. The term refers to the rules which courts apply when regulating the powers of the state.
B. The term refers to a guiding principle regarding how the powers of the state are regulated.
C. The term is a historical term that categorises cases regarding the powers of the state.
D. The term refers to the sanctions which a court can apply if they find that the government has abused their power.
E. The term refers to an academic theory regarding categorising the powers of the state.

Question 2

Ethelred is a member of the royal family and is fourth in line of succession to the throne of the United Kingdom. However, whilst driving on the public highway, he is stopped by the police for using his mobile phone whilst in charge of a motor vehicle, which is an offence under The Road Vehicles (Construction and Use) (Amendment) (No. 2) Regulations 2022.

Can Ethelred be charged with an offence under The Road Vehicles (Construction and Use) (Amendment) (No. 2) Regulations 2022?

A. No, Ethelred cannot be charged with an offence as the royal family are immune from prosecution.
B. Yes, Ethelred can be charged as the law applies equally to all, regardless of their royal credentials and status.
C. Yes, Ethelred can be charged but only if he agrees to submit to the court.
D. Yes, Ethelred can be charged but only if all ongoing proceedings are held in public.
E. No, Ethelred cannot be charged as the police have no jurisdiction over the royal family.

Question 3

HHJ Fingers is a serving district judge based in the North of England. She wishes to stand as a candidate in the Dunny-on-the-Wold by election, with the aim of becoming a Member of Parliament. It is her wish to remain as a judge whilst sitting as an MP.

Would this be possible or desirable under the British constitution for the judge to have her wishes?

A. Yes, because if elected she would be able to bring a legal perspective to the role of MP which would help in the design of new legislation.
B. Yes, because the principle of free and fair elections allows the constituency to elect whichever candidate they wish to represent them.
C. No, because holding both roles would be a potential abuse of power.
D. No, because if elected she would not be able to devote enough time to properly carry out her duties as either a judge or an MP.
E. No, because there would be a clear conflict of interest if, once elected, one of her constituents appeared before her in court.

PART 4 Judicial Review

4 Judicial Review and Access to the Courts

4.1 SQE Syllabus

The SQE1 syllabus requires students to demonstrate an awareness of a wide range of aspects of judicial review. These include the nature and process involved, the remedies that judicial review can provide, the grounds that can be used, and the decisions that can be challenged. In this chapter we will be looking to follow on from Chapter 3's consideration of how institutions hold each other accountable to now look at how the general public can use the law to ensure protection of individual freedoms.

4.2 Chapter Overview

Within this chapter we will look at the process of judicial review on a step-by-step basis considering each aspect of how claims can be made under this form of legal action.

We will consider the powers, the process, the heads of claim, and the remedies that can result.

4.3 What Is Judicial Review?

A judicial review is a process by which the decisions, acts, and omissions of a public body can be challenged. It is a court procedure that is typically heard before the Administrative Division of the High Court.

DOI: 10.4324/9781032642024-9

Under a judicial review procedure, it is the role of the High Court judges to examine the specific decision that has given rise to the claim, with a view to reaching an outcome as to whether the law has been correctly followed by the public body in question.

When a public body is created, the legislation that brings the body into existence will typically define the powers, duties, and process that the body should employ when making decisions. It is these parameters that act as the rule book by which decisions will be judged in a judicial review.

The process follows the expected requirements of a hearing in that there will be a claimant, who is seeking to challenge the decision of the public body, and a defendant, the public body who has made the decision. However, there will often be additional parties to a judicial review that will comprise others who may be affected by the outcome that the court reaches in the matter at hand.

Before we consider the judicial review process in detail, it is important to note the interaction between judicial review and the rule of law, the separation of powers, and parliamentary sovereignty.

- The rule of law and judicial review.

As noted previously, the rule of law is a guiding principle that represents equality before the law, whilst providing a check on the power of the executive over the general public. Judicial review has a key role to play in ensuring that individual freedoms are protected whilst ensuring that the executive cannot escape from legal responsibility should their exercise of power be on an unlawful basis.

- We have observed how the separation of powers works to ensure that power is balanced across the executive, the legislature, and the state. One key aspect of this balance is the use of judicial review as a means for the judiciary to oversee how the executive uses the powers that have been provided to it by the legislature.
- Finally, it is important to see how judicial review ensures that parliamentary sovereignty is upheld. As we have noted, the doctrine of parliamentary sovereignty requires that Parliament can pass any statute that it wishes, and this is not questioned within the process of judicial review. However, statute often grants powers to public bodies and judicial review ensures that the body in question only uses the powers that Parliament intended it to wield.

4.3.1 Overview of the Process

Figure 4.1 Stages within a judicial review

4.4 Accessing the Courts for Judicial Review

Before any matter can be brought before the court, it is vital that an assessment is made as to whether the claim itself has a sufficient basis to proceed upon. This requires consideration of four factors:

- Is the matter one of public law?
- Is the sufficient interests or 'standing' test met?
- Is the claim defeated by ouster provisions?
- Is the claim within time?

Is the Matter One of Public Law?

Whilst a powerful legal device, it should be noted that the scope of a judicial review is limited from the outset. When a judicial review is sought, it is not the role of the court to remake a decision or to even enquire as to the merits of the decision made. Instead, the court's role is to review the process under which the decision was made from which the decision itself may be ruled to be flawed and may then be revoked.

With the process of judicial review operating to assess the decisions of public bodies, it is only bodies who are exercising public law functions who are susceptible to challenge.

Is the Sufficient Interests or 'Standing' Test Met?

As directed by section 31(3) of the Senior Courts Act 1981, for a party to be able to bring an application for judicial review, it must be shown that the party has 'sufficient interest in the matter to which the application relates'.

The test for sufficient interest has been viewed by the courts in a wide manner to include both personal standing (where the individual is directly impacted by the decision requiring review) and also representative standing (where a group represent a section of society or a specific public interest).

The leading case on standing is provided by *R v Inland Revenue Commissioners ("IRC"), ex parte (1) National Federation of Self-Employed and (2) Small Businesses Ltd* [1982] AC 617. In the case judgment two principles aid in deciding whether a party has sufficient standing.

1) When determining standing, a wide range of factors may be taken into account including the duties in question, the nature of any alleged breach, and the proper construction and interpretation of the statute; and
2) The issue of standing and the merits of a case should typically be viewed as a whole, and this may require consideration of the entire legal and factual context to determine whether standing is established.

Subsequent case law has further developed the guidance available on determining sufficient interest to now require the courts to:

1) Confer standing on a party unless 'the applicant has no interest whatsoever, and is a mere busybody'. So if there exists an arguable case and no other factors bar the case progressing, then standing is established and the case should proceed to a substantive hearing.

2) The acceptance of standing is a matter for the court and the court alone to decide. So even if the parties to a case are in agreement to proceed, it is the court who has the final say on whether sufficient interest is present.
3) The question of standing permeates the case at all stages and this would include when any relevant remedy is considered.

The recent case of *The Queen (on the application of (1) Good Law Project Limited (2) Runnymede Trust) v (1) The Prime Minister (2) Secretary of State for Health and Social Care* [2022] EWHC 298 (Admin), whilst confirming that any calls to narrow the sufficient interests test should be resisted, did suggest that courts and defendants should more actively engage with the issue of standing. It is yet to be seen how this may lead to changes in future cases.

Is the Claim Defeated by Ouster Provisions?

Ouster clauses are specific provisions that are entered into legislation to prevent the decisions of public bodies from being challenged via the process of judicial review.

The justification for such clauses can be found in the doctrine of parliamentary supremacy, with Parliament able to restrict the jurisdiction of the courts if it chooses to do so.

When a judicial review is put before the courts to consider, and when an ouster clause is in place, the court has three options available to it when considering how to proceed. The court either can accept the clause and the claim will be defeated at that point or can utilise a device known as a constitutional 'parry' or, in extreme case, can use the constitutional 'lunge'.

The constitutional parry is a process under which the court subjects the ouster clause to very strict scrutiny. If the clause demonstrates a firm, clear, and explicit demonstration that it is the will of Parliament that there should be no judicial review, then the judge will apply the clause and the claim will fall. However, the separation of powers doctrine does allow the court to be able to use a narrow construction of the clause under which it may preserve the possibility of judicial review.

It is also possible for the court to simply decide that the clause does not apply to the specific issue raised within the case as a means to allow the process to proceed.

Whilst the 'parry' could be seen as judicial deflection, it should be noted that the constitutional 'lunge' involves a far more open challenge. As noted by Lord Carnwath in *R (on the application of Privacy International) v Investigatory Powers Tribunal and others* [2019] UKSC 22, the courts may be able to directly confront the ouster where the courts are prevented from providing their supervisory jurisdiction over possible abuses of power. However, this was mentioned in obiter and there has not yet been a requirement for the lunge to be employed.

Is the Claim Within Time?

Under CPR 54.5, claims for judicial review must typically be brought promptly and, in any event, within three months of the date on which the issue upon which the case rests arose. The whole approach of the CPR in this area is one of prompt action, in the case of *R (Paul Jones) v Chief Constable of Merseyside Police* [2017] EWHC 1816 (Admin), the court emphasised that the three-month period should be considered a backstop and actions should be commenced at the earliest juncture.

It should be noted that a judicial review of a planning matter should be brought within six weeks of the decision being made.

4.4.1 Parties Against Whom a Claim Can Be Made

As we have considered earlier, a judicial review is a procedure where the court considers the lawfulness of a decision made, or action taken, by a public body. This could also include consideration of a public body's failure to make a decision or take action as well.

It is important to therefore be aware of what a public body is.

Public bodies who can have decisions challenged include:

- Government ministers and departments – such as the Department for Work and Pensions, the Department for Education, and the Ministry of Defence
- Local authorities and local NHS trusts
- Maintained schools and school governing bodies
- Regulatory and supervisory bodies – such as the Care Quality Commission and the Charity Commission
- Chief constables and prison governors
- Magistrates', coroners', and county courts

4.4.1.1 Public and Private Bodies

Whilst an action for judicial review may only be brought against a body that is carrying out a public function, it should be noted that where a private organisation carries out a public function, it could also be subject to the process of judicial review.

The test that is applied can be found in Part 54 of the Civil Procedure Rules, which states that a claim for judicial review means:

> a claim to review the lawfulness of a decision, action or failure to act in relation to the exercise of a public function.

However, it should be noted that beyond this, there is no statutory definition of the term 'public function'.

We are therefore reliant on judicial interpretation of what a function of a public nature may be.

The most authoritative case is the judgment in *R v Panel on Takeovers and Mergers, ex p Datafin plc and another* [1987] 2 WLR 699. This case established that the court should consider the nature of a body's power and not just the source of that power in seeking to determine whether a public function was being exercised. For example, was the power contractual, statutory, or from royal prerogative?

In addition, the judgment suggests that consideration should be given to the type of activity that the body was engaged in.

The factors from Datafin have received subsequent consideration by the courts, and this has provided the following additional guidance.

- **Where a statutory power exists**

Where a body is created or governed by statute or has been given special statutory powers then it is usually the case that they will be considered to be performing a public function.

- **Where the arrangement is contractual**

The existence of a contract is viewed as a strong indication that the dispute is a private rather than a public matter.

- **Where the function is deemed as inherently private**

In cases such as *R v Disciplinary Committee of the Jockey Club, ex p Aga Khan* [1993] 1 WLR 909, *R v Football Association Ltd, ex p Football League Ltd* [1993] 2 All ER 833, and *Law v National Greyhound Racing Club Ltd [1983]* 3 All ER 300, it has consistently been stated that sporting organisations will be deemed to be private in nature.

Similarly, the cases of *R v Chief Rabbi of The United Hebrew Congregations of Great Britain and the Commonwealth, ex p Wachmann* [1992] 1 WLR 1036 and *R v Imam of Bury Park Mosque, Luton, ex p Ali (Sulaiman)* [1994] COD 142 demonstrate that religious bodies will also typically be viewed as inherently private.

It should also be noted that in situations where a public body contracts out a particular service to a private body, these arrangements will usually be considered as public in nature and therefore subject to judicial review. This was confirmed in the case of *YL v Birmingham City Council* [2007] UKHL 27.

4.4.1.2 Public Authority Under Human Rights

It is important to note that a different approach is taken in matters that allege a breach of a human right by a public authority. This requires consideration of section 6 of the Human Rights Act 1998 which states:

1) It is unlawful for a public authority to act in a way which is incompatible with a Convention right.
2) Subsection (1) does not apply to an act if –
   a) as the result of one or more provisions of primary legislation, the authority could not have acted differently; or
   b) in the case of one or more provisions of, or made under, primary legislation which cannot be read or given effect in a way which is compatible with the Convention rights, the authority was acting so as to give effect to or enforce those provisions.
3) In this section 'public authority' includes –
   a) a court or tribunal, and
   b) any person certain of whose functions are functions of a public nature, but does not include either House of Parliament or a person exercising functions in connection with proceedings in Parliament.
4) In subsection (3) 'Parliament' does not include the House of Lords in its judicial capacity.
5) In relation to a particular act, a person is not a public authority by virtue only of subsection (3) (b) if the nature of the act is private.
6) 'An act' includes a failure to act but does not include a failure to –
   a) introduce in, or lay before, Parliament a proposal for legislation; or
   b) make any primary legislation or remedial order.

It is therefore unlawful for a public authority to act in a manner that is incompatible with a right protected under the European Convention of Human Rights.

Again, the legislation relates to public authorities, which includes a range of organisations including the courts and tribunals. However, it should be noted that Parliament is not considered to be a public authority under the Human Rights Act.

For a body to be considered to be a core public authority, the courts tend to look at whether the body is:

- Publicly funded.
- Accountable to government.
- Supervised by government.
- Carrying out an inherently private role.
- Fixed with a public interest obligation.

We shall now proceed to consider the next step in the process, namely the grounds on which a judicial review can be commenced.

4.5 Grounds for Judicial Review

In the case of *CCSU v Minister for Civil Service* [1984] UKHL 9, Lord Diplock identified the three grounds upon which a domestic judicial review could be commenced. These grounds are:

- Illegality;
- Irrationality; and
- Procedural impropriety.

Illegality and irrationality are often considered to be the substantive grounds for review as they focus on the substantive elements that underpin the decision upon which judicial review is sought.

Procedural impropriety, as the name suggests, focusses on whether the correct procedure has been followed in the process of reaching the decision that is now subject to review.

It should be noted that whilst the aforementioned grounds are considered as domestic grounds for judicial review, there are also two further grounds for claim that are considered as the 'European' grounds. These focus upon either a breach of the European Convention of Human Rights or a breach of retained EU law.

We will now consider the aspects of each of the domestic grounds in detail.

4.5.1 Illegality

Illegality as a ground for judicial review is fundamentally a consideration of whether the identified public authority has acted inside or outside the scope of their legal powers.

It would therefore be correct to see illegality as a wider term that encompasses a number of different occurrences that can be subject to a judicial review.

4.5.1.1 *Simple* Ultra Vires

Any consideration of whether illegality has taken place in the making of a public authorities' decision requires consideration of the concepts of *intra vires* and *ultra vires*.

Whilst *intra vires* refers to an act that has taken place that is within a public authority's powers, *ultra vires*, translated from the original Latin phrase, simply means 'outside the power'.

It follows that if a decision has been made by an authority who does not hold the power to make that decision, then the action would be illegal.

However, consideration of *ultra vires* and illegality can be a little more complicated when we review case law upon the subject.

The issue is that pre–Lord Diplock's decision in *CCSU v Minister for Civil Service* [1984] UKHL 9, the term *ultra vires* was used as a 'catch-all' term that would be stated within judgments without reference to a specific ground. Within the more modern judgments we will now see the use of *ultra vires* as being the outcome of the case should illegality, irrationality, or procedural impropriety have occurred.

In the process of judicial review, we now consider the most straightforward form of illegality to be 'simple *ultra vires*'. Simple *ultra vires* occurs when a public body makes a decision that is beyond the scope of the powers held by that body.

In matters of simple *ultra vires*, the key factor for the courts in assessing the case is consideration of the original statute that granted the public body the powers used in making the decision. It is clear that the courts will see the wording of the statute as the expression of Parliament's will.

As Laws LJ stated in the case of *R (Cart) v Upper Tribunal* [2009] EWHC 3052 (Admin):

> If the meaning of statutory text is not controlled by such a judicial authority, it would at length be degraded to nothing more than a matter of opinion. Its scope and content would become muddied and unclear. Public bodies would not, by means of the judicial review jurisdiction, be kept within the confines of their powers prescribed by statute. The very effectiveness of statute law, Parliament's law, requires that none of these things happen.

The process of judicial review, regarding simple *ultra vires*, would involve the analysis and interpretation of wording and whilst this may seem a simple task, it has often been the case that this has proven a difficulty for the courts.

The cases of *Attorney-General v Fulham Corporation* [1921] 1 Ch 440 and *White and Collins v Minister of Health* [1939] 2 KB 838 demonstrate the issues that courts faced with defining terms that may seem simple, such as 'wash-house' or 'park'.

A more recent example of a public body acting in a manner deemed as simple *ultra vires* can be found in the case of *R v Richmond-upon-Thames LBC, ex p McCarthy and Stone (Developments) Ltd* [1992] 2 AC 48.

In the case, Richmond-upon-Thames Council had passed a resolution in July 1985 that enabled a charge of £25 to be levied in responding to enquiries made regarding development proposals. Pre-application consultation had been encouraged by the Secretary of State in paragraph 6 of Circular No. 22/80.

In August of the following year, the council charged the fee to the developer McCarthy and Stone for 'pre-application planning advice'. This took the form of an informal consultation between planning officers and the developer and subsequently the developer brought a claim to the High Court for a judicial review claiming that the charge had been levied without legal authority.

The House of Lords found for the developer, stating that the charges imposed were *ultra vires* as the council lacked the relevant power.

4.5.1.2 Fettering Discretion

A general principle that applies in matters of public law is that once a public body has been provided with a discretionary power, the courts will not allow that public body to restrict or 'fetter' that discretionary power.

In practice, fettering can occur in two ways:

1) Where the public body does not utilise the power themselves but acts under the direction of another; or
2) Where the public body applies a policy which unduly restricts the exercise of the discretionary power.

We shall consider each of these in turn.

ACTING UNDER THE DIRECTION OF ANOTHER

The key case on this subject is the case of *Lavender & Sons Ltd v Minister of Housing and Local Government* [1970] 1 WLR 1231. In the case, the claimant sought permission to extract sand and gravel from agricultural land. The permission was refused. In the letter confirming the refusal, the minister stated that he would not grant permission for extraction of sand and gravel 'unless the Minister for Agriculture is not opposed' to the proposed extraction. As the Minister for Agriculture had not indicated his approval for the works, permission had not been granted.

The claimant sought judicial review of the rejection and the court found in Lavender & Sons' favour, stating that although the minister was able to formulate a general policy, it was clear here that a decision that was within his powers had been fettered by his decision to take into account a fellow minister's view.

POLICIES THAT UNDULY RESTRICT THE EXERCISE OF A DISCRETIONARY POWER

The key case can be found in the matter of *British Oxygen v Minister of Technology* [1971] AC 610.

In this case, the claimant sought grants from the Board of Trade towards the £4 million that had been spent on the purchase of gas cylinders. The gas cylinders had been purchased at a cost of £20 each. Under the Industrial Development Act 1966, the Board of Trade possessed a discretionary power to award grants that assisted companies with capital expenditure. However, the policy of the Board of Trade was not to provide grants for items that cost less than £25. Therefore, under the terms of the Board of Trade's own policy, British Oxygen's claim for the grant was rejected.

The case was heard by the House of Lords, and the law lords held that while the Board of Trade did have the right to formulate its own general policy, the policy itself should not tie the hands of the Ministry from considering applications on a case-by-case basis.

Lord Reid stated:

> There may be cases where an officer or authority ought to listen to a substantial argument reasonably presented urging a change of policy. What the authority must not do is to refuse to listen at all. But a Ministry or large authority may have had to deal already with a multitude of similar applications and then they will almost certainly have evolved a policy so precise that it could well be called a rule. There can be no objection to that, provided the authority is always willing to listen to anyone with something new to say.

4.5.1.3 Delegation of Powers

The case of *Vine v National Dock Labour Board* [1957] AC 488 confirms that once Parliament has granted decision-making powers to a public body, those powers cannot then be sub-delegated further.

In the *Vine* case, the plaintiff was a registered dock worker who was employed, under the Dock Workers (Regulation of Employment) Order 1947, as a reserve dock worker. The scheme was operated via a series of local boards who had a range of powers, including the power to give seven days' notice of termination of employment to any dock worker who failed to comply with the terms of the scheme.

A complaint was made against Vine, alleging that he had failed to be on time for work on a regular basis. To deal with this, the local board appointed a committee to deal with the complaint. This committee subsequently terminated Vine's employment. Vine subsequently brought a claim, and the House of Lords found in his favour reaching the view that the plaintiff's purported dismissal was void as the local board had no power to delegate its disciplinary functions to the committee.

Lord Somervell commented:

> In deciding whether a 'person' has power to delegate, one has to consider the nature of the duty and the character of the person. Judicial authority normally cannot, of course, be delegated. . . . There are . . . many administrative duties which cannot be delegated.

It should be noted that there are two important exceptions to the rule regarding delegation of a power.

THE CARLTONA PRINCIPLE

In the case of *Carltona v Commissioners of Works* [1943] 2 All ER 560, Carltona Limited were faced with their factory being requisitioned by the government during the Second World War.

The factory owners sought a judicial review to challenge the legality of the factory requisition on the grounds that the order for requisition had been signed by a civil servant and not by the Minister for Works and Planning.

In finding against Carltona, Master of the Rolls, Lord Greene stated:

> In the administration of government in this country the functions which are given to ministers (and constitutionally properly given to ministers because they are constitutionally responsible) are functions so multifarious that no minister could ever personally attend to them . . . [therefore] The duties imposed upon ministers and the powers given to ministers are normally exercised under the authority of ministers by responsible officials of the department. Public business could not be carried on if that were not the case.

Confirming the view that under the convention of individual ministerial responsibility, the fact that the order had been signed by a civil servant rather than the minister had no bearing on the legality of the order. It was an acceptable form of delegation as government ministers are ultimately responsible to Parliament for the operation of and decisions made by their department.

SECTION 101 LOCAL GOVERNMENT ACT 1972

As per section 101(1) of the Local Government Act 1972:

> Subject to any express provision contained in this Act or any Act passed after this Act, a local authority may arrange for the discharge of any of their functions –
>
> a) by a committee, a sub-committee or an officer of the authority; or
> b) by any other local authority.

This allows a further exception to the rule of delegation as long as the local authority passes a formal resolution that confirms the delegation of decision-making powers in this manner.

4.5.1.4 *Improper Purposes*

The decision of a public body taken for improper purposes may also fall foul of the test for illegality.

In the case of *Trafford v Blackpool Borough Council* [2014] EWHC (Admin), the claimant was a solicitor who had brought a number of claims against Blackpool

Borough Council. The claimant's firm, North Solicitors, were based at the New Blackpool Enterprise Centre, a building that was owned by Blackpool Borough Council.

At the time when the lease was due for renewal, the defendant took the decision to not allow the renewal and a claim was brought with the court finding that the decision to not renew was invalid due to the improper exercise of discretion.

4.5.2 Irrationality and Proportionality

One of the most well-known grounds on which to challenge the decision of a public body is the ground of irrationality.

The Wednesbury Principle

The Wednesbury principle derives from the judicial approach expounded in the case of *Associated Provincial Picture Houses Ltd v Wednesbury Corporation* [1948] 1 KB 223.

In the case, Associated Provincial Picture Houses was granted a licence to operate a cinema in Staffordshire. The licence was granted on condition that no child under the age of 15 would be admitted to the cinema on a Sunday. The cinema operators challenged the decision on the grounds of it being unreasonable.

The court decided that it had no power to issue a writ quashing the decision, simply because the court did not agree with the condition imposed. Instead the court proposed that if it were going to rule against public bodies to have been unreasonable, the decision-makers would have to be shown to have:

1) Given undue relevance to facts that in reality were not of relevance to the matter at hand.
2) Given no consideration to relevant information that should have been considered in the decision-making process.
3) Made a decision, the like of which was so unreasonable that no reasonable decision-maker would have reached that view.

In the case at hand, the court ruled that the corporation's conduct was not inappropriate and complied with the relevant law.

As Lord Greene MR said:

> It is true the discretion must be exercised reasonably. Now what does that mean? Lawyers familiar with the phraseology commonly used in relation to exercise of statutory discretions often use the word 'unreasonable' in a rather comprehensive sense. It has frequently been used and is frequently used as a general description of the things that must not be done. For instance, a person

> entrusted with a discretion must, so to speak, direct himself properly in law. He must call his own attention to the matters which he is bound to consider. He must exclude from his consideration matters which are irrelevant to what he has to consider. If he does not obey those rules, he may truly be said, and often is said, to be acting 'unreasonably.' Similarly, there may be something so absurd that no sensible person could ever dream that it lay within the powers of the authority. Warrington LJ in Short v Poole Corporation [1926] Ch. 66, 90, 91 gave the example of the red-haired teacher, dismissed because she had red hair. That is unreasonable in one sense. In another sense it is taking into consideration extraneous matters. It is so unreasonable that it might almost be described as being done in bad faith; and, in fact, all these things run into one another.

The principles and tests outlined in Wednesbury stood unaltered until the case of *CCSU v Minister for Civil Service* [1984] UKHL 9.

The case involved the use of the royal prerogative to ban employees of the Government Communications Headquarters (GCHQ), from joining a trade union on the basis that this would be a threat to national security.

The House of Lords decision in the case was that whilst decision made using the royal prerogative was subject to judicial review, in this case the action of restraining employees from joining a trade union was valid.

In regards to Wednesbury, it was the judgment of Lord Diplock that applied, during which he stated:

> By 'irrationality' I mean what can by now be succinctly referred to as 'Wednesbury unreasonableness'. It applies to a decision which is so outrageous in its defiance of logic or of accepted moral standards *that no sensible person who had applied his mind to the question to be decided could have arrived at it.* Whether a decision falls within this category is a question that judges by their training and experience should be well equipped to answer, or else there would be something badly wrong with our judicial system. To justify the court's exercise of this role, resort I think is today no longer needed to Viscount Radcliffe's ingenious explanation in *Edwards v Bairstow* [1956] AC 14 of irrationality as a ground for a court's reversal of a decision by ascribing it to an inferred though unidentifiable mistake of law by the decision-maker. 'Irrationality' by now can stand upon its own feet as an accepted ground on which a decision may be attacked by judicial review.

The reframed test outlined within Lord Diplock's judgment made a difficult test to meet, one that may seem impossible. However, more recent decisions have shown that the bar can be reached.

In *Wheeler v Leicester City Council* [1985] AC 1054, Leicester Rugby Union Club had been granted the right to use a recreation ground that was owned by the city council.

Three players from Leicester were subsequently selected for a tour of South Africa that was to be held during the apartheid era. At the time Leicester City Council were opposed to any sporting links with South Africa. When the club did not subsequently stop the players from going on the tour the council took the step of banning the club from using the recreation ground.

The club brought a subsequent action under judicial review and were successful, with Lord Roskill stating:

> Persuasion, even powerful persuasion, is always a permissible way of seeking to obtain an objective. But in a field where other views can equally legitimately be held, persuasion, however powerful, must not be allowed to cross that line where it moves into the field of illegitimate pressure coupled with the threat of sanctions . . . [thus] the actions of the council were unreasonable in the Wednesbury sense.

In 2018, a further example was provided in the case of *R (DSD & Anor) v The Parole Board of England and Wales* [2018] EWHC 694 (Admin).

The case involved the 'Black Cab Rapist' John Worboys and the direction of the Parole Board to release him from custody. The court upheld the challenge to the release and took the step of quashing the direction to release citing the failure of the Parole Board to undertake further inquiry. Of particular interest was that Worboys had admitted to only 12 sexual offences, whereas evidence suggested that he had been involved in more than 80.

The ground of proportionality has developed from the ground of irrationality.

In claims that typically centre upon Human Rights or EU law, it may be necessary for the Administrative Court to decide whether an act or decision was a proportionate means of achieving a legitimate aim.

In essence, a claim under this heading may allow the courts to quash the exercising of discretionary powers, where there is no reasonable relation between the objective which is sought to be achieved and the means used to reach that end. This can also be extended to circumstances where the punishments imposed by administrative bodies or courts are considered to be wholly out of proportion to the relevant misconduct.

The question of proportionality was discussed in detail during the case of *Pham v Secretary of State for the Home Department* [2015] UKSC19. In this case the

Supreme Court showed clear support for the ground to be available in matters of judicial review.

The confirmation of the validity of this ground is hugely significant. However, the comments were *obiter*, but they do outline a standalone ground that would provide an easier test to achieve than many other approaches taken to judicial review.

4.5.3 Procedural Impropriety

The final ground to consider is the ground of procedural impropriety, which again flows from Lord Diplock's judgment in the case of *Council of Civil Service Unions v Minister for the Civil Service* [1984] UKHL 9.

Lord Diplock described procedural impropriety in the following manner:

> I have described the third head as 'procedural impropriety' rather than failure to observe basic rules of natural justice or failure to act with procedural fairness towards the person who will be affected by the decision. This is because susceptibility to judicial review under this head covers also failure by an administrative tribunal to observe procedural rules that are expressly laid down in the legislative instrument by which its jurisdiction is conferred, even where such failure does not involve any denial of natural justice.

As can be observed here, procedural impropriety has a series of elements. These elements were developed into a series of six principles by Lord Mustill in the case of *R v Secretary of State for the Home Department, ex p Doody* [1994] AC 531. These are as follows:

1) Where an Act of Parliament confers an administrative power there is a presumption that it will be exercised in a manner which is fair in all the circumstances.
2) The standards of fairness are not immutable. They may change with the passage of time, both in general and in their application to decisions of a particular type.
3) The principles of fairness are not to be applied by rote identically in every situation. What fairness demands is dependent on the context of the decision, and this is to be taken into account in all its aspects.
4) An essential feature of the context is the statute which creates the discretion, as regards both its language and the shape of the legal and administrative system within which the decision is taken.
5) Fairness will very often require that a person who may be adversely affected by the decision will have an opportunity to make representations on his own behalf either before the decision is taken with a view to producing a favourable result; or after it is taken, with a view to procuring its modification; or both.

6) Since the person affected usually cannot make worthwhile representations without knowing what factors may weigh against his interests, fairness will very often require that he is informed of the gist of the case which he has to answer.

Whilst the principles provide a useful starting point in considering procedural impropriety, it is important to consider the context in which the principles will apply.

The starting point to consider is that in the majority of cases, where an Act of Parliament confers a decision-making power to a public body, it will also state the requirements as to the process required in reaching a decision.

At the same time, it is important to note that not every failure to correctly follow a procedure will immediately invalidate the decision made. If the courts are presented with a case where they are required to assess a procedural defect within the decision-making process, the starting point will always be to consider the requirements of the relevant legislation.

If the departure from legislation is so gross as to warrant the voiding of the decision, then this is deemed as a mandatory invalidation. If the departure from the procedure outlined in the legislation is less serious, then the issue is deemed as directory. The term simply means that whilst there exists a failure, that failure in itself is not sufficient to void the decision.

4.5.3.1 Natural Justice

As part of the process of ensuring that fair decisions are made, it is important to consider the requirements of natural justice. This can be summarised under two broad headings, namely the right to be heard and the rule against bias.

4.5.3.2 Right to Be Heard

The right to be heard is an ancient principle that has application in many branches of the legal process.

The key case on the right to be heard can be found in the judgment in *Ridge v Baldwin* [1964] AC 40. The *Ridge* case extended the doctrine of natural justice into the realm of administrative decision-making.

In the case, Ridge was employed as the Chief Constable of Brighton Police. During the course of his employment, Ridge, along with two other officers, had been arrested and charged with conspiracy to obstruct the course of justice.

During the course of the trial, the judge raised serious doubts about Ridge's fitness to hold the office of Chief Constable. Despite this he was acquitted of the charge.

Subsequently, the Brighton Watch Committee, who had oversight of the Brighton Police under the leadership of George Baldwin, took the decision to dismiss Ridge without allowing him the opportunity of a hearing or even any notice as to their decision. Ridge appealed, arguing that the committee had acted unlawfully in terminating his appointment in this manner.

The House of Lords ruled that the decision of the committee had violated the doctrine of natural justice.

In his leading judgment, Lord Reid stated that the right to be heard:

> goes back many centuries in our law and appears in a multitude of judgments of judges of the highest authority. In modern times opinions have sometimes been expressed to the effect that natural justice is so vague as to be practically meaningless. But I would regard these as tainted by the perennial fallacy that because something cannot be cut and dried or nicely weighed or measured therefore it does not exist . . . It appears to me that one reason why the authorities on natural justice have been found difficult to reconcile is that insufficient attention has been paid to the great difference between various kinds of cases in which it has been sought to apply the principle. What a minister ought to do in considering objections to a scheme may be very different from what a watch committee ought to do in considering whether to dismiss a chief constable.

Following the judgment in *Ridge*, the ruling has been applied in a range of cases including in *Re HK* [1967] 2 QB 617, *McInnes v Onslow-Fane* [1978] 1 WLR 1520 and *Bank Mellat v Her Majesty's Treasury* [2013] UKSC 39.

Once a party has established that they are entitled to a hearing, it then becomes a matter for the court to determine what form the hearing should take with a view to ensuring that fairness is maintained. Whilst largely dependent on the nature of the issues involved, consideration would be given to whether an oral hearing is required, whether disclosure is required by the parties, whether there will be the right to examine and cross-examine witnesses, and whether legal representation will be permitted.

4.5.3.3 Rule Against Bias

The second element of natural justice to consider is the rule against bias.

The rule against bias provides that a decision-maker should have no personal interest in the outcome of a decision. This rule has two sub-considerations, namely those of direct and indirect interest.

DIRECT INTERESTS

A direct interest is where the individual decision-maker is personally linked to an aspect of the decision being made. The existence of direct interests has been observed across a range of cases involving interest.

In *Dimes v Grand Junction Canal Proprietors* (1852) 10 ER 301, it was confirmed – not unexpectedly – by the House of Lords that any notion of financial gain to the decision-maker falls within the direct interest category.

In *R v Bow Street Metropolitan Stipendiary Magistrate and Others, ex p Pinochet Ugarte* (No 2) [2000] 1 AC 119, the impartiality of Lord Hoffman was questioned as part of his role in the House of Lords decision to deny former Chilean dictator General Augusto Pinochet immunity as a former sovereign from arrest and extradition to Spain. The case found against the former leader only for it to come to light later on that Lord Hoffman, who had been part of a 3–2 majority decision, had been an unpaid director and chairman of Amnesty International Charity Ltd. Although there was never any question of financial gain in this case, it was ruled that his non-pecuniary interest was sufficient to allow the original decision to be overturned.

INDIRECT INTERESTS

An example of an indirect interest would be where a family member of the decision-maker had an interest in the decision reached in the case. With these being indirect rather than direct, any finding of impropriety does not automatically result in the decision being quashed. Instead the court is required to investigate the matter prior to then reaching a decision on whether to void the decision.

The leading case on this area is the case of *Porter v Magill* [2002] 2 AC 357.

In the case Dame Shirley Porter, the Conservative Party Leader of Westminster Council, adopted a policy to sell council houses in parts of the council area where it was believed that those who would benefit from the policy were more likely to vote Conservative.

Magill was the auditor who was given the responsibility of investigating the claims that an abuse of power had been perpetrated. However, prior to the completion of the investigation, Magill took the step of calling a press conference at which he announced that the initial investigation was suggestive of a finding against Dame Porter.

It subsequently transpired that she was found guilty and fined.

However, she chose to appeal the decision on the grounds that Magill had pre-empted his own investigation findings and had therefore made the decision a *fait accompli*. In other words he put pressure on himself to find a decision of guilt.

The court found against Dame Porter. They ruled that although the press conference was an unwise action, there was no evidence to suggest that Magill had unwittingly created an indirect interest in the outcome of his own investigation.

instrument, then this would have the effect of invalidating all actions and decisions that had been taken under the authority of that statutory instrument.

If a quashing order is granted, then the court can send the case back to the original decision-maker with directions to remake the decision in light of the court judgment. Alternatively, although rarely applied, the court can dispense with the return of the matter to the decision-maker and can make the decision itself.

Nevertheless, the quashing order is the most common order that is made by the courts at the conclusion of a successful judicial review case.

4.7.1.2 Prohibiting Order

A prohibiting order has similarities to a quashing order in that both prevent the decision-maker from acting beyond the scope of their powers. The key difference is that a prohibiting order prevents future actions of the decision-maker, converse to the quashing order's retrospective effect.

These tend to be a rarely used order as it is often the case that claimants prefer the ordinary remedy of an injunction. One example of the use of a prohibiting order was in the case of *R v Liverpool Corporation, ex p Liverpool Taxi Fleet Operators' Association* [1972] 2 QB 299, as discussed previously.

4.7.1.3 Mandatory Order

A mandatory order compels a public authority to fulfil their duty. So whilst quashing orders and prohibiting orders deal with a wrongful exercise of power, a mandatory order addresses the failure of a decision-maker to act. Examples of where mandatory orders may be used can be observed in a range of matters, such as the failure of an authority to assess a disabled person's needs, a failure to approve building plans, or a failure to improve the conditions of confinement.

It should be noted that mandatory orders are often used in conjunction with quashing orders.

4.7.2 Ordinary

In addition to the range of specific remedies for judicial review matters – the prerogative orders – there also exists a number of alternative remedies through the application of a number of private law remedies that can be provided.

4.7.2.1 Declaration

A declaration is a court order that confirms the respective legal positions of the parties. The use of a declaration does not in itself change the legal positions. However, they do have a useful function in public law matters.

As an example, the case of *Royal College of Nursing v Department of Health and Social Security* [1981] AC 800 shows how the declaration can operate to resolve a dispute. In the case, the government issued guidance that stated that nurses could lawfully perform part of the procedure involved in the termination of a pregnancy. The claimants disputed the guidance and a declaration was sought to confirm that the guidance was incorrect.

The government in turn counterclaimed, requesting a declaration that the guidance was correct.

The outcome of the case was a declaration confirming that the guidance was in fact correct.

4.7.2.2 Injunction

The use of the private law remedy of an injunction is an alternative to the use of a prohibiting order. The purpose of an injunction is to stop a body from taking what would be an illegal action.

The benefit of using an injunction, rather than the prohibiting order, is that as well as there being the remedy of a final injunction, there also exists the possibility of gaining an interim injunction which can assist in preventing a decision from being put into effect whilst the court considers the case and provides a final adjudication. The approach is regularly used in matters of asylum, in which a deportation order can be prevented using an interim injunction, allowing the court the time to consider whether the deportation decision was correct.

4.7.2.3 Damages

It should be noted that there is no general right to damages available to successful claimants in judicial review matters. However, a discretion is available to the courts to award damages under section 31(4) of the Senior Courts Act 1981.

The discretion applies when the judicial review claim is aligned with a further cause of action. For example, where the matter under judicial review also demonstrates a breach of a statutory duty or demonstrable misfeasance in public office or where the facts give rise to a private action in tort.

So, should a decision-maker make a decision that takes into account an irrelevant consideration, this will likely provide sufficient grounds for the quashing of the erroneous decision on the ground of illegality. This may then allow the aggrieved party to bring an action against the official, should the decision have been made incorrectly as a result of malice.

The ability of the court to address both matters simultaneously is designed to allow resolution of all matters without the need to commence parallel proceedings.

4.8 Reform of Judicial Review

The Judicial Review and Courts Act 2022 has introduced a number of reforms into the conduct of judicial reviews. The changes have the effect of broadening the range of remedies that the courts may choose to award whilst at the same time there are limits applied to the use of judicial review as a means to appeal against the ruling of tribunals.

The changes that impact upon remedies are as follows:

- Section 1 of the act makes changes to the use of quashing orders. Under the act, the courts now have the option of suspending the quashing orders with a view to allowing the public body to correct any failure that has been identified by the court. This attempts to mitigate the substantial retrospective effect of quashing orders.

As an example, the new legislation would be useful in limiting the liability of tax-payers. Under current legislation, a quashing order reframes the situation to a position where it is as if the decision had never occurred. This has the potential to impact thousands or millions of people who could then be entitled to damages.

The new approach would limit the retrospective effects of any judgment to just those who had issued a claim before the date of the judgment.

- Section 2 of the act removes the Administrative Court as an option for those seeking to challenge decisions of the Upper Tribunal. This may be subject to legal challenge on the grounds that it appears a clear restriction on access to justice.

Chapter 4 Revision Points

This chapter has introduced the reader to the stages and requirements that comprise a judicial review process. We have the basis of the claim, the available grounds, the procedure for commencing and progressing the claim, and the remedies that are available to the successful claimant.

We have also observed how judicial review interacts with the previous structures and how the process of judicial review continues to evolve.

Multiple Choice Questions

Question 1

The fictitious Morals in Entertainment Act provides local authorities with the power to grant licences to concert venues in their area 'on any conditions that the local authority deems appropriate'. Under the act, Dunny-on-the-Wold Council grants IPB Events a licence on condition that no act shall appear at the venue unless approval is first obtained from the local morality committee of the local church group. IPB Events objects to this condition.

Which of the following options best describes whether IPB can successfully seek judicial review of the licence condition?

A. It is possible for IPB Events to successfully seek judicial review as the delegation to the local morality committee was in breach of the rule against delegation.
B. It is possible for IPB Events to successfully seek judicial review as the decision breaches the ground of illegality, as the licensing authority has delegated decision-making power to a body which is neither a civil servant nor a local authority committee or officer.
C. It is possible for IPB Events to successfully seek judicial review as the council, by delegating decision-making power in this manner, falls under the ground of illegality due to an unreasonable purpose.
D. It is not possible for IPB Events to successfully seek judicial review as the decision is lawful and the council is able to delegate decision-making power to the local morality committee and the delegation cannot be subject to challenge.
E. It is not possible for IPB Events to successfully challenge the decision as the decision is lawful with the delegation made to a local committee and therefore the statutory exception relating to local bodies will apply.

Question 2

The fictitious "Onerous Powers of the State Act" states that all decisions by local authorities 'shall not be called into question in any legal proceedings whatsoever'. ZFK Enterprises wants to challenge a local authority decision that has impacted upon the business. The process of bringing a claim is brought two months after the decision was made. ZFK Enterprises waited for two months, as they were busy securing further supply contracts for their product range. However, they have now decided to bring an application as they feel that there are valid grounds for challenge.

Is the company likely to be successful in bringing a claim for judicial review of the decision?

A. ZFK Enterprises is unlikely to successfully bring the claim as, despite the ouster clause failing to prevent a challenge being brought against the decisions of the local authority, there has been undue delay on the part of the company in lodging the claim, without a valid reason.
B. ZFK Enterprises is unlikely to successfully bring the claim as the ouster clause is sufficient to protect the local authority's decision from challenge and there has been undue delay on the part of the company in lodging the claim, without a valid reason.
C. ZFK Enterprises is unlikely to successfully bring the claim as the ouster clause is sufficient to protect the local authority's decision from challenge even if the claim is lodged within the three-month time limit.
D. ZFK Enterprises is likely to successfully bring the claim as the ouster clause does not protect the local authority from being challenged and the claim will be lodged without undue delay on the part of the company.
E. ZFK Enterprises is likely to successfully bring the claim as the ouster clause does not protect the local authority from being challenged and the claim will be made within the three-month time limit.

Question 3

A woman has applied to Dunny-on-the-Wold Council for a licence to run a bar and restaurant within the town. The council has the statutory power to provide licences for bars and restaurants within their area. The council has confirmed that they are not going to consider her application and as a result of being unable to trade she has lost money.

What remedy or remedies should the woman apply for?

A. A mandatory order and damages.
B. A mandatory order.
C. Damages.
D. A quashing order.
E. A quashing order and damages.

PART

5

Human Rights, Public Order, and Retained EU Law

5 The Human Rights Act 1998

5.1 SQE Syllabus

The SQE1 syllabus requires that an individual has an awareness of the Human Rights Act 1998, and more specifically, sections 2, 3, 4, 6, 7, 8, and 10. It is also important to have knowledge of some of the individual articles contained within the European Convention on Human Rights.

5.2 Chapter Overview

This chapter will provide a broad understanding of the articles contained within the European Convention on Human Rights, and how the Human Rights Act 1998 has given effect to the European Convention on Human Rights as a crucial facet of the English legal system.

5.3 What Are Human Rights?

Human rights are those rights that exist simply because we exist as humans. They can be further described as universal and applicable to all humans notwithstanding their individual characteristics pertaining to their sex, religion, and nationality, to name a few. They are the fundamental series of norms that are necessary in any civilised society.

It is important to note that there are differences between civil liberties and human rights. Civil liberties are individual to a country and are rights that are allocated to citizens of a state and can be withdrawn (certainly from a UK position), by repeal via statute. Civil liberties are not alien to the UK, and we can see an establishment of such liberties in our rich legal history, penning back to the Magna Carta in 1215. Historically, such liberties can also be seen in the form of section 1 of Habeas Corpus Act 1679, the Bill of Rights 1689, and the Reform Acts of the 19th and 20th centuries. These 'liberties' are designed to discourage governments/executive institutions from abusing their powers through interference.

DOI: 10.4324/9781032642024-11

5.4 The European Convention on Human Rights

The European Convention on Human Rights is an international treaty that was adopted by the Council of Europe in 1950. It sets out a comprehensive framework for the protection of human rights and fundamental freedoms in Europe. The convention consists of a preamble and 59 articles, which cover a wide range of rights and liberties.

These rights are conveyed upon citizens and form one of three types of rights: absolute rights, limited rights, and qualified rights.

5.4.1 Absolute Rights

These rights are considered sacrosanct from a dignity and humanity perspective and cannot be denied to anybody. It is important to note that a state cannot derogate from absolute rights and must be applied unqualifiedly with no limitations. For example, Article 3 ensures that every citizen is free from torture.

5.4.2 Limited Rights

These rights are capable of limitation, if expressly permissible by the law. Thus, in certain circumstances, a right that is conveyed upon an individual can be interfered with legally. For example, Article 5 contains the right to liberty and security. The law allows for liberty to be interfered with in the event of being convicted of a crime.

5.4.3 Qualified Rights

These rights are those that can be infringed in certain circumstances, for example infringement of rights may be in the public interest and/or if it is to protect an individual's rights. Commonly, we see examples of this when a newspaper reporter, whom under Article 10 has the right to freely express themselves, writes a story on an individual, whom under Article 8 has the right to respect for private life. Similarly, a public authority could prohibit a right-wing political party from protesting, thus infringing their rights of a freedom of assembly. This is often a balancing exercise between the rights of the parties involved.

5.4.3.1 How Is Interference With Qualified Rights Justified?

A public authority's interference into qualified rights must successfully navigate a tripartite test.

- Firstly, any interference with any qualified rights must be supported by a clear basis in law. To this extent, there must be a clear and ascertainable law that governs the interference with the convention right. These could be in the form of statutes, regulations, and common law.[1] The case of Malone v Metropolitan Police Commissioner (no2) [1979] Ch 344 and Malone v UK [1984] 7 EHRR 14 is

1 Even the rules and policies of a professional body could amount to 'law' – see *J Council v (1) GU (2) A NHS Trust (3) Care Quality Commission (4) X Limited* (11845015) (2012) EWHC 3531 (COP) and *Munjaz v UK* (17 July 2012) Application Number: 2931/06.

an excellent example of when interference takes place without a basis in law. The court found that the applicant's rights under Article 8 had been breached due to his phone being 'bugged' by the police. Interestingly, the decision by the European Court of Human Rights in Malone led to the enacting of the Interception of Communications Act 1985, which provided a clear basis and prescription in law for future telephone surveillance.

- Secondly, any interference must pursue a legitimate aim. A legitimate aim includes national security, prevention of crime, and protection of public health, amongst others.
- Thirdly, any interference must be proportionate and necessary in a democratic society. That is to say, the interference must go no further than what is required to achieve the legitimate aim. This can sometimes be described as the state not using 'a sledgehammer to crack a nut'.

In summary, the test for proportionality can be seen as follows:[2]

1. Whether the legislative objective is sufficiently important to justify the limiting of a fundamental right;
2. Whether the measures in place are rationally connected to the objective;
3. Whether a less intrusive measure could have utilised;
4. Whether a fair balance has been struck between the rights of the individuals and interests of the community.[3]

5.4.4 The Doctrine of the Margin of Appreciation

The doctrine of the margin of appreciation guarantees that all contracting states uphold a minimal standard of human rights protection, while also permitting some room for variation based on the unique characteristics of each jurisdiction. From a jurisprudential perspective, the doctrine of the margin of appreciation and its importance in balancing the convention rights and a state's room for manoeuvre in the application of the convention cannot be understated.

One example of this can be seen in the case of *Handyside v United Kingdom* (1976) 1 EHRR 737.

The case concerned the publication of the *Little Red Schoolbook* intended for schoolchildren, which contained a chapter on sexual intercourse and related topics. The Obscene Publications Act was utilised in order to seize the books, followed by an order that prohibited any further publications against the publishers. Handyside was also convicted of possessing obscene publications for monetary gain and was subsequently fined. The European Court of Human Rights agreed

2 This was a three-stage test in *R (on the application of Daly) v Secretary of State for the Home Department* [2001] UKHL 26, [2001] 2 AC 532, *Huang v Home Secretary* [2001] UKHL 11. However, see Lord Sumption's judgment at para 20 in *Bank Mellat v Her Majesty's Treasury* (no2) [2013] UKSC 39.

3 Per Lord Sumption at paragraph 20 – *emphasis added.*

that there was an interference with his Article 10 rights, but this was prescribed by law, pursued a legitimate aim, and the interference was necessary in a democratic society.

The Handyside ruling from 1976 provided the initial explanation of the margin of appreciation. There, the European Court of Human Rights made it clear that there is a process involved in guaranteeing human rights: firstly, national courts evaluate whether national measures are compatible with the convention, and that states would be left with a *margin of appreciation* in interpreting whether a particular measure was necessary, and then the European Court of Human Rights reviews this assessment, if required.

5.5 The Convention Rights

5.5.1 Article 2 – Right to Life (Absolute Right)

Article 2 of the European Convention on Human Rights guarantees the right to life. It states:

1) Everyone's right to life shall be protected by law. No one shall be deprived of their life intentionally, except in the execution of a sentence of a court following their conviction of a crime for which this penalty is provided by law.
2) Deprivation of life shall not be regarded as inflicted in contravention of this article when it results from the use of force which is no more than absolutely necessary:
   a) in defence of any person from unlawful violence;
   b) in order to effect a lawful arrest or to prevent the escape of a person lawfully detained;
   c) in action lawfully taken for the purpose of quelling a riot or insurrection.

Table 5.1 A table showcasing the articles and their respective categories

Absolute rights	Limited rights	Qualified rights
Article 2 – Right to life	Article 4 – Freedom from slavery (Part 2 only)	Article 8 – Right to respect for private and family life
Article 3 – Freedom from torture	Article 5 – Right to liberty and security	Article 9 – Freedom of thought, conscience, and religion
Article 4 – Freedom from slavery (Part 1 only)	Article 6 – Right to a fair trial	Article 10 – Freedom of expression
Article 7 – No punishment without the law		Article 11 – Freedom of assembly and association

This article is extremely relevant when considering the limitation of state power in the context of life. It not only forbids killing by the state that is considered arbitrary, but also extends to the use of force by the police, the law with respect to abortion and when it can be carried out, and whether one can also be assisted to take their own life. Furthermore, it specifies situations in which using force that results in death can be acceptable, like self-defence and preventing an escape from prison. It is, however, important to note that any force used in this instance must be no more than that which is absolutely necessary.

Pretty v United Kingdom *(2002) (Application No 2346/02, 29 April 2002)*

The article was examined in the landmark end of life case. The applicant, who was suffering from motor neurone disease and wished to end her life, sought permission seeking immunity for her husband in the event he assisted her in ending her life. Such assistance in committing suicide would be contrary to section 2 of the Suicide Act 1961 and would be construed as unlawful. Following an application for judicial review and subsequent appeal to the UK courts, her request was rejected. She made an application to the European Court of Human Rights citing Article 2 allowing an individual to decide whether to live or die. She also sought to rely upon Article 8, which protected a right to respect her private life. Regarding Article 2, this was rejected by the European Court of Human Rights, who stated that the right to life could not be interpreted as also giving the right to die. With respect to Article 8, there was also no violation, as the interference by the state in using the Suicide Act 1961 in prohibiting her husband from assisting her was deemed to be a necessary interference which was in accordance with the law and also necessary in a democratic society.

5.5.2 Article 3 – Torture, Inhumane or Degrading Treatment (Absolute Right)

Article 3 of the European Convention on Human Rights states:

> No one shall be subjected to torture or to inhuman or degrading treatment or punishment.

The prohibition of torture and inhuman or degrading treatment is an absolute right, meaning that there are no circumstances in which it can be justified or limited.

It is important to note that the interpretation and application of Article 3 has evolved through case law, with the European Court of Human Rights providing guidance on the scope and standards of protection under this provision. The court has interpreted 'torture' as involving intentional and severe physical or mental suffering, while 'inhuman or degrading treatment' refers to treatment that causes serious humiliation, degradation, or suffering but falls short of torture.

States have an obligation to prevent and investigate any allegations of torture or inhuman or degrading treatment within their jurisdiction. If a violation of Article 3 is established, the court may order compensation for the victim and require the state to take measures to prevent similar violations in the future.

It is important to note that the article also prohibits a state from deporting an individual to another state whereby they would be in danger of persecution whether publicly or privately. If it can be shown that a deportation risked treatment that would violate Article 3, then such a deportation would not be obliged under the European Convention on Human Rights. Such an interpretation of the article results in individuals being allowed to remain in a country.

Ireland v United Kingdom *(1980) 2 EHRR 25*

This case revolves around the treatment of Republican Army personnel and the treatment that was administered to them. The techniques utilised caused suffering and consisted of sleep and food deprivation. The court adjudged that whilst not torture, inhumane and degrading treatment was inflicted, thus violating Article 3.

Chahal v United Kingdom *(1997) 23 EHRR 413*

This matter involved a Sikh family of which Mr Chahal had entered the UK illegally in 1971. He was granted indefinite leave to stay after applying in 1973. In 1984, he visited India, whereby he attended events at the golden temple; he was involved in arranging resistance in the movement for an autonomous Punjab. Here, he was arrested by the police and was detained for 21 days, whereby he was beaten unconscious, electrocuted, and subjected to a mock execution. He was then released without charge.

In October 1985, Mr Chahal was detained under UK terrorism laws on suspicion of seeking to assassinate the Indian Prime Minister on his visit to the country. The government was also concerned about his connections with a proscribed terrorist group in India. The state subsequently sought to deport Mr Chahal thereafter. Following the Home Secretary's refusal to grant political asylum, the matter was contested in the European Court of Human Rights, where the court considered evidence that the applicant would be subjected to torture or death in the event he was deported. The court held that notwithstanding the threat to national security, such a deportation would violate Mr Chahal's rights under Article 3 of the convention, due to evidence that the Indian authorities were complicit in violating convention rights.

This case demonstrates that even whereby individuals are not seen as law-abiding members of the public and the government would prefer them to be deported, the likelihood of a violation of the individual's rights in another jurisdiction could be enough to prevent such a deportation under the European Convention on Human Rights.

5.5.3 Article 4 – Prohibition of Slavery and Forced Labour (Absolute Right)[4]

Article 4 of the European Convention on Human Rights prohibits slavery, servitude, and forced labour. It states:

1) No one shall be held in slavery or servitude.
2) No one shall be required to perform forced or compulsory labour.
3) For the purpose of this article, 'forced or compulsory labour' shall not include:
   a) Any work required to be done in the ordinary course of detention imposed according to the provisions of Article 5 of this Convention or during conditional release from such detention.
   b) Any service of a military character or, in case of conscientious objectors in countries where they are recognized, service exacted instead of compulsory military service.
   c. Any service exacted in case of an emergency or calamity threatening the life or well-being of the community.
   d. Any work or service which forms part of normal civic obligations.

The exclusions stated in paragraph 3 make it clear that while some jobs or services might be mandated by law in some special situations, they should not be viewed as forced or compulsory labour. For example, jobs that are carried out by prisoners are seen as being a part of their rehabilitation. Further, compulsory military service would also not be deemed as forced or compulsory labour. Even roles that are deemed to be civic, such as jury service, would not be classed as forced or compulsory labour.

CN v United Kingdom *(2013) 56 EHRR 24*

The victim in this matter complained that upon arrival into the jurisdiction, she was forced to work, and her passport and earnings were taken. The European Court of Human Rights decided that a violation of Article 4 had taken place due to an absence of criminal protection for the victim, which meant that the police investigation into her complaint was ineffective. Prior to the judgment being handed down in 2012, changes to the law did take place, with the introduction of section 71 of the Coroners and Justice Act 2009, which included a section on slavery, servitude, and forced or compulsory labour.[5]

5.5.4 Article 5 – Right to Liberty and Security (Limited Right)

1) Everyone has the right to liberty and security of person. No one shall be deprived of his liberty save in the following cases and in accordance with a procedure prescribed by law:

4 This refers to 4(1) only, as 4(2) would come under limited rights.

5 Omitted by the Modern Slavery Act 2015.

a) the lawful detention of a person after conviction by a competent court;
b) the lawful arrest or detention of a person for non-compliance with the lawful order of a court or in order to secure the fulfilment of any obligation prescribed by law;
c) the lawful arrest or detention of a person effected for the purpose of bringing him before the competent legal authority on reasonable suspicion of having committed an offence or when it is reasonably considered necessary to prevent his committing an offence or fleeing after having done so;
d) the detention of a minor by lawful order for the purpose of educational supervision or his lawful detention for the purpose of bringing him before the competent legal authority;
e) the lawful detention of persons for the prevention of the spreading of infectious diseases, of persons of unsound mind, alcoholics or drug addicts or vagrants;
f) the lawful arrest or detention of a person to prevent his effecting an unauthorised entry into the country or of a person against whom action is being taken with a view to deportation or extradition.

2) Everyone who is arrested shall be informed promptly, in a language which he understands, of the reasons for his arrest and of any charge against him.
3) Everyone arrested or detained in accordance with the provisions of paragraph 1(c) of this Article shall be brought promptly before a judge or other officer authorised by law to exercise judicial power and shall be entitled to trial within a reasonable time or to release pending trial. Release may be conditioned by guarantees to appear for trial.
4) Everyone who is deprived of his liberty by arrest or detention shall be entitled to take proceedings by which the lawfulness of his detention shall be decided speedily by a court and his release ordered if the detention is not lawful.
5) Everyone who has been the victim of arrest or detention in contravention of the provisions of this Article shall have an enforceable right to compensation.

Article 5 of the European Convention on Human Rights plays a crucial role in safeguarding individuals' rights to liberty and security. It ensures that the state cannot arbitrarily detain individuals and provides important procedural safeguards to prevent abuse of power. Furthermore, it cannot be an absolute right as it has a list of exhaustive derogations as to when interference with the right is permissible. Again, examples of detention is not limited to police custody, but also for situations involving deportation matters, admissions to a mental hospital, and even where infectious diseases are likely to be spread.

Secretary of the State for the Home Department v JJ *[2007] UKHL 45*

In this matter, the Secretary of State utilised statutory powers to make orders against six individuals based upon suspicions that such individuals posed a risk of committing acts of terrorism. As such, the individuals were required to stay in a specific place, with an electronic tag, and could only visit areas specified as part of the order. Permission from the Home Office was required in the event they wanted to meet anybody.

The House of Lords decided that a violation of the individuals' liberty had taken place, and stated that the power to make an order rested with the court, and the 'Secretary of State has no power to make an order that imposes any obligation incompatible with article 5'.[6]

5.5.5 Article 6 – Right to a Fair Trial (Limited Right)

1) In the determination of his civil rights and obligations or of any criminal charge against him, everyone is entitled to a fair and public hearing within a reasonable time by an independent and impartial tribunal established by law. Judgment shall be pronounced publicly but the press and public may be excluded from all or part of the trial in the interests of morals, public order or national security in a democratic society, where the interests of juveniles or the protection of the private life of the parties so require, or to the extent strictly necessary in the opinion of the court in special circumstances where publicity would prejudice the interests of justice.
2) Everyone charged with a criminal offence shall be presumed innocent until proved guilty according to law.
3) Everyone charged with a criminal offence has the following minimum rights:
    a) to be informed promptly, in a language which he understands and in detail, of the nature and cause of the accusation against him;
    b) to have adequate time and facilities for the preparation of his defence;
    c) to defend himself in person or through legal assistance of his own choosing or, if he has not sufficient means to pay for legal assistance, to be given it free when the interests of justice so require;
    d) to examine or have examined witnesses against him and to obtain the attendance and examination of witnesses on his behalf under the same conditions as witnesses against him;
    e) to have the free assistance of an interpreter if he cannot understand or speak the language used in court.

This article provides fundamental rights that are necessary to ensure that the judicial process is fair for all individuals. This is enshrined with common principles such as the presumption of innocence (or innocent until proven guilty), procedural rights and fairness (especially in the criminal trial process and procedure), and the permissibility of a court to disallow the press and public from trials.

6 Per Lord Bingham of Cornhill at para 27.

Consideration of Judicial Fairness Was Considered in the Matter of Runa Begum v Tower Hamlets LBC *[2003] UKHL 5*

The applicant was homeless and was offered accommodation under section 202 of the Housing Act 1996. However, the accommodation was not suitable for her due to it being in an area that was described as a drug abuse and racism hotspot. An appeal was raised and following a review by the Local Authority, it was decided that the offered accommodation was reasonable. The applicant challenged the procedure invoked for reviewing the offered accommodation, on the basis that the Local Authority were in fact reviewing themselves. In the House of Lords, Lord Bingham suggested that substantial procedural safeguards existed, and a fair review process could take place notwithstanding the fact that the reviewer may not be deemed as an 'independent and impartial tribunal'. Considering the scope of Article 6(1), the court determined that the reviewer's decision did not violate Ms Begum's civil rights under Article 6(1).

5.5.6 Article 7 – No Punishment Without Law (Absolute Right)

Article 7 of the European Convention on Human Rights states:

1) No one shall be held guilty of any criminal offence on account of any act or omission which did not constitute a criminal offence under national or international law at the time when it was committed. Nor shall a heavier penalty be imposed than the one that was applicable at the time the criminal offence was committed.
2) This Article shall not prejudice the trial and punishment of any person for any act or omission which, at the time when it was committed, was criminal according to the general principles of law recognised by civilised nations.

In 3.4, we considered the rule of law and its importance in a functioning legal system and society at large. Article 7 promotes the notion of the principle of legality and the principle of non-retroactivity (criminal law). By its very nature, it crucially protects from punishments for acts which were not crimes at the time they were committed and the application of the law retrospectively. It also ensures that any sanctions or punishment are not harsher than those already in place.

R v Secretary of State for the Home Department Ex Parte Uttley *[2004] UKHL 38*

Here, the respondent was convicted of a crime in 1995 that was committed in 1983. He complained that a change in the law taking place after the crime had been committed resulted in a more stringent punishment. Namely, he would be released on licence instead of his sentence simply expiring. He was sentenced for a total of 12 years imprisonment, and the consequences of being sentenced in 1995 differed to that of 1983. The release protocol of prisoners was altered by the Criminal Justice Act 1991. As such, were he to have been sentenced pre-1991, then upon the completion of two-thirds of his sentence, he would have been released (subject to good behaviour), and the sentence would have expired. Due to the provisions inserted by the 1991 act, a prisoner would be released following the completion of two-thirds of the sentence but would be released on licence, the terms of which would not expire until three-quarters of the sentence had been completed. The terms of the licence also placed a number of restrictions on the respondent's freedoms.

He complained that such a change violated his rights under Article 7(1). The court ruled that there was no violation of Article 7(1), as the sentence passed was not heavier than what the law would have permitted (life imprisonment) whether the sentence was passed in 1983 or 1995. Further, the release of a prisoner after competing two-thirds of the sentence and being released on licence *mitigated rather than augmented* the severity of the sentence.[7]

5.5.7 Article 8 – Right to Respect for Private and Family Life (Qualified Right)

1) Everyone has the right to respect for their private and family life, their home, and their correspondence.
2) There shall be no interference by a public authority with the exercise of this right except as is in accordance with the law and is necessary in a democratic society in the interests of national security, public safety, or the economic well-being of the country, for the prevention of disorder or crime, for the protection of health or morals, or for the protection of the rights and freedoms of others.

Article 8 encompasses a range of personal and family related matters, which include, but are not limited to, rights to privacy, rights to establish and maintain a family, and the rights to control personal information. Its application ranges to both individuals and families and can be invoked when there is interference with a person's private life by the government, surveillance, data protection, and immigration cases involving family life. See discussion at 5.4.3.1 as to how an interference for this right can be justified.

Peck v United Kingdom *[2003] EHRR 287*

The applicant was recorded by Brentwood Borough Council with the use of CCTV, which was then released to the public to showcase the benefits and effectiveness of CCTV and its use thereof. However, the footage captured was of the applicant with a knife, seeking to attempt suicide. Still images and footage were shown by newspapers and television outlets. Following complaints to a number of regulatory bodies, he applied for judicial review of the council's disclosure of the footage to media outlets, which had no basis in law. The application was rejected, and the subsequent appeal to the Court of Appeal was also dismissed on the grounds that the Criminal Justice and Public Order Act 1994 permitted the local authority to provide CCTV footage to promote preventions of crime.

7 Per lord Phillips of Worth Matravers, paragraph 28.

The applicant filed a claim at the European Court of Human Rights and complained that the release of the footage was a violation of his right to a private life under Article 8. The European Court of Human Rights held that a violation of the applicant's Article 8 rights had occurred. The *ratio* focussed on the fact that the applicant's identity had not been effectively masked, and the aftermath of the suicide attempt had been recorded and disclosed to the public. It is important to note that Article 8 is a qualified right, and interference can be justified. Accordingly, as the local authority had the statutory power to distribute CCTV footage in the prevention of a crime, the interference had a legal basis and pursued a legitimate aim. In terms of necessity and proportionality, the test was not satisfied, as there were other options available to the local authority in the distribution of the CCTV, namely that of masking the identity or even gaining consent from the applicant via the police.

5.5.8 Article 9 – Freedom of Thought, Conscience, and Religion (Qualified Right)

1) Everyone has the right to freedom of thought, conscience and religion; this right includes freedom to change his religion or belief and freedom, either alone or in community with others and in public or private, to manifest his religion or belief, in worship, teaching, practice and observance.
2) Freedom to manifest one's religion or beliefs shall be subject only to such limitations as are prescribed by law and are necessary in a democratic society in the interests of public safety, for the protection of public order, health or morals, or for the protection of the rights and freedoms of others.

Eweida v United Kingdom *[2013] ECHR 37*

The applicant (and three others) applied to the European Court of Human Rights for a decision based upon the United Kingdom failing to protect their rights under Article 9 of the European Convention on Human Rights. They complained that the law failed them in protecting their rights in manifesting their religion and beliefs. Ms Eweida was a devout Christian and wore a cross on a chain, which contravened British Airways' uniform policy. She was suspended from her job, and then returned after British Airways changed their uniform policy but refused to compensate her for loss of earnings during her suspension period. The Court of Appeal also rejected her claim for indirect discrimination under the Employment Equality Regulations 2003. The European Court of Human Rights agreed with the applicant and stated that the domestic authority had failed to protect her right to manifest her religion in violation of Article 9. She was awarded compensation and costs.

5.5.9 Article 10 – Freedom of Expression

1) Everyone has the right to freedom of expression. This right shall include freedom to hold opinions and to receive and impart information and ideas without interference by public authority and regardless of frontiers. This article shall not prevent States from requiring the licensing of broadcasting, television or cinema enterprises.

2) The exercise of these freedoms, since it carries with it duties and responsibilities, may be subject to such formalities, conditions, restrictions or penalties as are prescribed by law and are necessary in a democratic society, in the interests of national security, territorial integrity or public safety, for the prevention of disorder or crime, for the protection of health or morals, for the protection of the reputation or rights of others, for preventing the disclosure of information received in confidence, or for maintaining the authority and impartiality of the judiciary.

This provision is one that is routinely prevalent and frequently utilised not just in the media, but also in day-to-day life. Article 10 protects a broad range of expressions, including political opinions, artistic and cultural expressions, and commercial speech. The term 'expression' includes views and opinion (both spoken and published). Examples of this can be seen in newspaper stories involving celebrities and the use of injunctions to stop media outlets from publishing stories about such celebrities.

However, it also recognises that certain limitations can be imposed on the freedom of expression in specific circumstances, and these limitations must be prescribed by law and necessary in a democratic society. See discussion at 5.4.3.1 as to how an interference for this right can be justified.

The Observer and The Guardian v United Kingdom *(1992) 14 EHRR 153*

The applicants published details of the Spycatcher book after gathering information and details from its author. The book revolved around memoirs of the author, who was previously employed by the British government in Intelligence. Injunctions were granted by the English courts, notwithstanding the fact that the book had been published in other jurisdictions such as the United States. The applicant newspapers applied to the European Court of Human Rights and submitted that the injunctions were a violation of Article 10. The court considered whether interference of Article 10 by the injunction was prescribed by law, whether the aims of the interference were legitimate, and whether the interference was necessary in a democratic society to ensure that interests of national security were protected. They came to the conclusion that the injunctions did represent violations of Article 10.

Furthermore, the fact that the book had been published in the United States meant that the contents of the book were no longer confidential, and thus, the injunction was no longer a legitimate interference with Article 10.

5.5.10 Article 11 – Freedom of Assembly and Association (Qualified Right)

1) Everyone has the right to freedom of peaceful assembly and to freedom of association with others, including the right to form and to join trade unions for the protection of his interests.

2) No restrictions shall be placed on the exercise of these rights other than such as are prescribed by law and are necessary in a democratic society in the interests of national security or public safety, for the prevention of disorder or crime, for the protection of health or morals or for the protection of the rights and freedoms of others. This Article shall not prevent the imposition of lawful restrictions on the exercise of these rights by members of the armed forces, of the police or of the administration of the State.

It is important to note, that as with all other qualified rights, interference with such rights can take place. For assemblies, this will usually be done via public order law. See discussion at 5.4.3.1 as to how an interference for this right can be justified. The United Kingdom allows assemblies and protests as a fundamental right in a democratic society.

5.6 The Human Rights Act 1998 and Its UK Operation

It is important to note that the dualist nature of the UK constitution means that the convention alone has no legal force within the UK in its own right. The Human Rights Act 1998 gives effect to the European Convention on Human Rights, and all laws are now interpreted in a manner that gives effect to convention rights. The act does not create new rights, instead it allows existing convention rights found in Schedule 1 of the act to be enforced via the national courts against the state.

It is important to understand the operation of a number of sections of the act.

5.6.1 Section 2

Section 2 of the Human Rights Act requires a court to take into account any decisions of the European Court of Human Rights (and organs of the Council of Europe) when dealing with a matter in relation to a convention right.

It is, however, important to note that notwithstanding Article 46(1) of the European Convention on Human Rights, where contracting parties have provided an undertaking to abide by the final judgments of the court, the Human Rights Act 1998 does not require those decisions to be followed.[8]

Furthermore, it would not be possible for a judgment of the European Court of Human Rights to be enforced in a domestic court, and thus an individual may be relying on the state following the decision.[9]

8 *The Queen (on the Application of Elan-Cane) v The Secretary of State for the Home Department* [2020] EWCA Civ 363.

9 *Hirst v the United Kingdom* (no2) [2005] ECHR 681 relating to prisoner's voting rights.

5.6.2 Section 3

Section 3 of the Human Rights Act is perhaps the most interesting due to its inherent nature and what it is asking the courts to do.

Section 3 states:

1) So far as it is possible to do so, primary legislation and subordinate legislation must be read and given effect in a way which is compatible with the Convention rights.
2) This section-
    a) applies to primary legislation and subordinate legislation whenever enacted;
    b) does not affect the validity, continuing operation or enforcement of any incompatible primary legislation; and
    c) does not affect the validity, continuing operation or enforcement of any incompatible subordinate legislation if (disregarding any possibility of revocation) primary legislation prevents removal of the incompatibility.

To this end, it is clear that the courts have a duty to interpret legislation in a manner that makes it compatible with convention rights. This is an interpretation section of the act, and it is important to note that courts are *not* given the power to invalidate acts on the basis that they do not comply with convention rights. Section 1 clearly seeks to limit any inherent power to do so with the use of the phrase 'so far as is possible to do so'.

This issue was developed by Lord Steyn in *R v A (no. 2)* [2001] UKHL 25, who stated that the interpretative obligation under s3 of the 1998 Act is a strong one. It applies even if there is no ambiguity in the language . . . in accordance with the will of Parliament as reflected in s.3, it will sometimes be necessary to adopt an interpretation which linguistically 'may appear strained'.[10] Lord Hope took a more measured approach, stating that the section does not allow 'judges to act as legislators'.[11]

This section, especially when combined with Lord Steyn's judgment, promotes 'lawmaking from the bench', especially if the courts are going to interpret statutes in a manner where words can be 'linguistically' strained, potentially going against the intentions and will of Parliament (and thus, its supremacy), in order to ensure compliance with convention rights.

Ghaidan v Godin Mendoza *[2004] UKHL 30*

The Rent Act 1977 stated that a surviving spouse would automatically become a statutory tenant. This, however, was clearly written going from wife to husband, and vice versa.

10 Per Lord Steyn at para 44.

11 Per Lord Hope at para 108.

The issue in this matter arose whether the term 'wife or husband' could be read in a manner that was consistent with Article 8 and Article 14 (non-discrimination). The couple, who were in a long-term and stable same-sex relationship, sought to claim the succession of tenancy after the original tenant died, notwithstanding the wording in the Rent Act being explicit.

The court utilised their interpretative powers under section 3 in a manner that allowed the section in Rent Act 1977 to be compatible with convention rights, avoiding legislative intervention.

5.6.3 Section 4

Section 4 follows on from section 3, whereby if a court is unable to interpret the legislation in line with convention rights, then by virtue of Section 4(2), 'If the court is satisfied that the provision is incompatible with a Convention right, it may make a declaration of that incompatibility'.

Section 4, again, provides unique powers to the court, those which *prima facie* allow the court to issue a declaration of incompatibility under section 4(2). The question of parliamentary supremacy is once again raised, as whilst judges have been empowered by the act to issue a declaration of incompatibility (as a last resort), a declaration in itself can be perceived to be a de facto questioning of Parliament and their lawmaking, given the act in question is incompatible with the convention but should be subordinate to convention rights.

It is important to note that an act is unaffected in the event a declaration of incompatibility is issued by the courts.[12] This is safeguarded in section 4(6) of the act, where it stated:

> 4(6) A declaration under this section ("a declaration of incompatibility")–
>
> A) Does not affect the validity, continuing operation or enforcement of the provision in respect of which it is given; and
>
> B) It is not binding on the parties to the proceedings in which it is made

Once the declaration has been issued, this will enable the executive and the relevant government minister in charge to make the necessary amendments in order to ensure compliance with the convention rights. This will be discussed further in section 5.6.7.

5.6.4 Section 6

Section 6 of the Human Rights Act is particularly important, as it prohibits public authorities from acting in a manner that is incompatible with a convention right. As per section 6(3), a public authority also includes a court or tribunal and any person whose functions are of a public nature.

12 *A and others v Secretary of State for the Home Department* [2004] UKHL 56 – Per Baroness Hale at para 220.

Procedurally, in order to pursue human rights matters against a public authority, an applicant will normally utilise the administrative courts via the medium of judicial review. As such, please refresh your memory by referring back to Chapter 4 for the judicial review process and 4.5.2 and 5.4.3.1 for the element of proportionality. The test of proportionality has been developed extensively in this regard, especially in relation to qualified rights and the justification of perceived interference of those rights by a public authority.

Horizontal Effect

The main objective of incorporation of convention rights was to allow individuals to enforce rights against state bodies (or public authorities as the Human Rights Act demotes). No specific provision was entered that allowed the convention rights to be enforceable between private individuals (horizontally). The effect of section 6, though, is not confined to those cases. Section 6 *could* have the effect of forcing the courts to develop new rights in existing causes of actions between individuals (or private companies), as the courts themselves are public authorities. Thus, they would be obliged to give effect to convention rights.[13] This was further elaborated in the breach of confidence matter of *Campbell v MGN Ltd*. [2004] UKHL 22, where the celebrity, Naomi Campbell, was photographed leaving a Narcotics Anonymous meeting, of which the photographs were published in a double spread in *The Mirror*. Campbell claimed for breach of confidentiality and compensation which was subsequently awarded compensation. Whilst the matter revolved around the established cause of action of breach of confidence and privacy, Article 8 and Article 10 rights were invoked by the parties. Lord Nichols stated:

> The time has come to recognise that the values enshrined in articles 8 and 10 are now part of the cause of action for breach of confidence. As Lord Woolf CJ has said, the courts have been able to achieve this result by absorbing the rights protected by articles 8 and 10 into this cause of action . . . Further, it should now be recognised that for this purpose these values are of general application. The values embodied in articles 8 and 10 are as much applicable in disputes between individuals or between an individual and a non-governmental body such as a newspaper as they are in disputes between individuals and a public.[14]

It is important to note that this continues to be a developing area of law; however, instances of Article 8 and the right to a private life can theoretically be invoked in matters involving, for example, landlord and tenant, employment, and family law matters that consist of established causes of action.

13 *Douglas v Hello* [2005] EWCA Civ 595.
14 Para 17.

5.6.5 Section 7

By virtue of section 7, sufficient interest/standing would be granted if the applicant were the victim of the alleged infringement. In terms of time limits, the period to bring an action would be one calendar year from the date on which the act took place. The court also has discretion to extend this period by virtue of section 7(5)(b) if the circumstances warrant.

As discussed in 5.6.4, the most common method to bring forth an action – due to the very reason that it involves a public authority – would be via an application for judicial review. This would be done by completing form N1, which allows an applicant to tick yes to the question 'Does, or will, your claim include any issues under the Human Rights Act 1998?'[15]

It is important to note that direct applications to the European Court of Human Rights is possible, but only to those who have *exhausted* all domestic remedies, and the matter must be substantially different from previously decided matters and should not be manifestly ill-founded.[16]

5.6.6 Section 8

Whilst damages can be awarded in human rights matters, it is important to note that the enactment of the Human Rights Act 1998 was never a tortious one, where liability and blame was to be apportioned, with successful claims resulting in compensatory awards. The crux of the act was to give effect to convention rights via domestic law.

In the event that damages are to be awarded, the courts must take into account the principles that have been applied by the European Court of Human Rights under Article 41 of the convention (which does not form part of Schedule 1 of the Human Rights Act).

5.6.7 Section 10

Section 10 is linked closely with section 4(2), if and when the court issues a declaration of incompatibility.

In such an event, a minister of the Crown is given power under 10(2) to make the necessary amendments in order to make the legislation compatible, by removing the incompatibility. This is done by making a 'remedial order'.

15 Please refer to Practice Direction 7A at 2.11 – (1) The normal rules apply in deciding in which court and specialist list a claim that includes issues under the Human Rights Act 1998 should be started. They also apply in deciding which procedure to use to start the claim; this Part or CPR Part 8 or CPR Part 54 (judicial review).

16 Applications requesting the courts retry a matter that has been concluded at a domestic court (unless they are arbitrary in their decision-making) and a lack of evidence.

5.6.8 Section 19

Ministers in charge of bills proceeding through Parliament are required to make a statement of compatibility to ensure that such a bill is compatible with convention rights.

5.6.9 Schedule 1, Human Rights Act 1998

Schedule 1 of the Human Rights Act can be found within the Human Rights Act.

Part 1 provides an overview of the convention rights that the act gives effect to.

Part 2 provides an overview of the First Protocol with regards to the protection of property, the right to education and the right to free elections.

Part 3 provides an overview of the Sixth Protocol, which abolishes the death penalty.

Chapter 5 Revision Points

- The Human Rights Act 1998 was enacted to give effect to convention rights into the legal system.
- Section 3 of the act is an interpretation section that allows the courts to interpret legislation in a manner that allows compliance with convention rights.
- Section 4 of the Human Rights Act allows a court to issue a declaration of incompatibility in the event it is unable to interpret an act in compliance with convention rights under section 3.
- The focus of the act is for individuals to bring action against infringement of convention rights against public authorities, which includes the courts under section 6.
- Convention rights can be split into absolute, limited, and qualified rights.
- With qualified rights, states are able to interfere with an individual's convention rights if such an interference can be justified. The courts have to balance the rights of one party with another in such an instance.
- A state must show when interfering with a convention right: there must be a clear basis in law, the interference is in pursuit of a legitimate aim, and the interference must be necessary and proportionate in a democratic society.

Multiple Choice Questions

Question 1

At what point can an application be made to the European Court of Human Rights?

A. An appeal must be made by either the Court of Appeal or the Supreme Court.
B. An application may be made to the European Court of Human Rights at any point.
C. An application may be made to the European Court of Human Rights after all procedures and remedies have been exhausted in domestic law.
D. A reference must be made by the Supreme Court to the European Court of Human Rights.
E. An application must be to a relevant higher court in order to get permission to apply to the European Court of Human Rights.

Question 2

The Court of Appeal is dealing with an appeal whereby a section in the (Hypothetical) Public Order Act 1997 is conflicting with a convention right.

Which option best describes the legal position?

A. Due to the supremacy of Parliament, the court simply must apply the act in its current format notwithstanding the conflict.
B. There is no requirement to give effect to the convention, given the European Court of Human Rights' judgments are not binding.
C. The courts must interpret the legislation so far as is it is possible to do so and give effect in a manner that is compatible with convention rights.
D. Due to the conflict, a declaration of incompatibility must be issued.
E. The Court of Appeal can refer the matter to the Supreme Court, who have the power to disapply infringing element of the act.

Question 3

Your client is a council tenant who has a tenancy agreement with private social housing company who have been contracted by the local council, who will subsidise a portion of your tenant's rent. Your tenant has come to you with concerns regarding breaches of convention rights. Section 6 of the Human Rights Act states that actions can only be brought against a 'public authority'.

Which option best describes a public authority?

A. Any person whose functions are functions of a public nature.
B. Any person whose functions are of and incorporate public services.
C. Any person whose functions are functions of a statutory nature.
D. Any person whose functions are functions of a governmental nature.
E. Any person whose functions are functions of a parliamentary nature.

6 Public Order Law and Offences

6.1 SQE Syllabus

The SQE syllabus requires knowledge of public order law, namely that of processions, assemblies, and breach of the peace.

6.2 Chapter Overview

This chapter will seek to build upon freedom of assembly that was discussed in Chapter 5 and allow you to consider the legal basis and when interference can be made in relation to processions and marches. It will also consider breach of the peace and other offences utilised in order keep public order.

6.3 The Public Order Act 1986

The English legal system has been built upon solid foundations over its rich history. From the Norman conquest onwards, the right for citizens to voice their discontent in a public manner has been sacrosanct. With this in mind, the Public Order Act 1986 was enacted which codifies the law and sought control over public processions, assemblies, and other related criminal activities in relation to public order.[1] This forms a key learning outcome of the SQE.

6.3.1 Processions

A procession can be defined as a march or a moving protest that takes place in a public place or highway or a place that public will have access to. When we think about processions, we can think back to some processions that have taken place more recently, such as Extinction Rebellion, Black Lives Matter, and even more recently, marches against war. Protests with numbers often going into the thousands cause a significant issue from a policing perspective, as with the sheer numbers involved, there are clear issues in relation to public safety and violence.

1 LAW COM No123, Criminal Law: Offence Relating to Public Order, 24 October 1983.

DOI: 10.4324/9781032642024-12

6.3.1.1 Notification of a Procession

By virtue of sections 11(1) and 11(3) of the Public Order Act 1986, advanced written notice must be provided six clear days in advance of any public processions that are designed to demonstrate support or opposition to the views and actions of other body or persons, to publicise a cause or campaign, or to mark or commemorate an event. Section 11(3) requires information such as date, time, proposed routes, and the information of those arranging the same.

Further, by virtue of section 11(4), such notices must be delivered to a police station or delivered via the postal system, although it is important to note the postal rule regarding service of documents being served when posted does not apply. It is also possible (and far easier) to provide notice via an online form, should a local police station accept. Greater Manchester Police for example, can be notified of a procession via their website.[2]

A failure to notify the police, or a deviation from the notified route, could result in the organising personnel being guilty of an offence and a fine under section 11(10). However, a defence does exist in the event the organiser can prove that they had no knowledge of the failure to satisfy the requirements of section 11(8). With regards to the procession deviating from an agreed route, it is a defence if they can prove that such a deviation was beyond their control (11(9).

When events are held regularly there is no requirement to provide written notification to the police. See *R (Kay) v Commissioner of the Police of the Metropolis* [2008] UKHL 69, where cyclists that rode in protest frequently in London were held to be a public procession, but its frequency of monthly protests had meant it had become customary, and hence forth, notification to the police under the Public Order Act 1986 was no longer required.

6.3.1.2 Imposing Conditions on a Procession

The police have a wide remit when it comes to imposing conditions on a procession, and these are done in the event they believe that a procession may lead to serious public disorder, property damage, or serious disruption to the life of the community. In England and Wales, this also extends to the noise created.[3]

In such instances, section 12 provides authority to the police to allow the procession subject to conditions, which can be based around the route of the procession, time limiting the procession, or prohibition of entry of the procession into certain areas. These conditions are capable of being imposed in advance or during the procession by the most senior officer present.

2 I'm planning a procession through a public area | Greater Manchester Police (gmp.police.uk).

3 As established by the Police, Crime, Sentencing and Courts Act 2022.

6.3.1.3 *Banning a Procession*

In the event that a procession is likely to lead to serious public disorder notwithstanding the application of conditions, then the power to prohibit the procession in its entirety may be exercised by virtue of section 13 of the Public Order Act 1986. The power of issuing such an order rests with the local council where the procession is to be held, and one may be granted for a period not exceeding three months. The local council may only make the order once consent has been granted by the Secretary of State. For processions in the City of London, such an order may only be granted by the Commissioner of the Police for the City of London or the Commissioner of Police of the Metropolis, again, after consent is provided by the Secretary of State.

It is important to note that an organiser who in contravention of such an order continues with a procession will commit an offence.

6.3.2 Assemblies

An assembly, in contrast to a procession, is a static gathering of more than two people within a public place in the open air. By virtue of section 16 of the Public Order Act 1986, a gathering can now also consist of a single person protest.[4] It goes without saying that the lack of movement in an assembly would make it easier for the police to manage, and as such, there are much more restricted police powers in terms of interference. An assembly can be both stationary and mobile. Amendments to assemblies in the Public Order Act 1986 have been made via recent legislation such as the Public Order Act 2023 and the Police, Crime, Sentencing and Courts Act 2022.

6.3.2.1 *Imposing Conditions on an Assembly*

Similar to public processions, conditions can be applied to assemblies by virtue of section 14 of the Public Order Act 1986. Like section 12, these conditions can be imposed on the basis of the senior officer being in reasonable belief of the likelihood of the assembly leading to serious public disorder. On this basis, it would be reasonable to impose such conditions such as that of limiting the number of people who take part, specifying the location and entry/exit points of the assembly itself, and applying a time limit to the assembly. These conditions can be applied by the senior ranking officer present at the assembly or the Chief Officer of police when notice of an intended assembly has been provided. It is also important to note that conditions can also be applied to one-person protests by virtue of the guidance in section 14ZA of the Public Order Act 1986.

It is important to note that any conditions imposed on processions and assemblies are susceptible to judicial review.

4 Section 14ZA as introduced within section 14 of the Public Order Act 1986 by the by Police, Crime, Sentencing and Courts Act 2022 (c. 32), ss. 79(1).

R (ON THE APPLICATION OF JONES) V COMMISSIONER OF POLICE FOR THE METROPOLIS (EXTINCTION REBELLION) [2019] EWHC 2957 (ADMIN)

It was held that conditions applied to an 'Extinction Rebellion Autumn Uprising' were beyond the powers/*ultra vires*. The court considered whether several public place 'sit-ins' constituted as a single public gathering, or series of different gatherings, and the interpretation of section 14 by the superintendent with the application of the condition of a ban on *all* Autumn Uprising assemblies and future assemblies in October 2019. It was argued by the respondent that they should be interpreted as being a *single* assembly – notwithstanding its different times and locations, given they were in relation to the same cause. The court deemed them to be assemblies in the plural sense of the word. Further, as clearly stated within the act, section 14 requires conditions to be made by the highest-ranking officer *present* at the assembly. No such public assembly had taken place at the time when the conditions were imposed, and the superintendent required presence at the future *public* assemblies in order for section 14 to be applicable.

To this end, it is important to note that unlike section 13, where there is power to prohibit processions, no such power exists for that of assemblies.

6.3.2.2 The Public Order Act 2023

The Public Order Act 2023, known as the 'anti-protest bill', was given Royal Assent on 2 May 2023 and introduces some additional offences from a public order perspective. New offences have been introduced for locking on, being equipped for locking on, tunnelling, being equipped for tunnelling, causing serious disruption by being present in a tunnel, in addition to obstructing major transport works and interfering with the use of key national infrastructure.[5]

Sections 20–29 allow for the granting of serious disruption prevention orders, to regulate and control protest-related offences.

6.3.2.3 Police, Crime, Sentencing and Courts Act 2022

Part 3 of this act focussed on public order and sought to introduce additional conditions within the Public Order Act 1986 that could apply to public processions and assemblies, namely that of noise generation that would result in serious disruption to the activities of an organisation (12aa and 14aa) or relevant significant impact of the noise on persons within the vicinity (12ab and 14ab).

6.3.2.4 Trespassory Assemblies

The Public Order Act 1986 also provides guidance on trespassory assemblies, which was inserted into the act by the Criminal Justice and Public Order Act 1994. Section 14A provides clarity of the law in relation to assemblies that are held on land of which the public have no or limited right of access. In such an instance, the

5 Sections 1–8 of the Public Order Act 2023.

Table 6.1 A table showcasing the differences between a procession and an assembly with example queries

Question?	Procession	Assembly
Is notification required?	Yes	No
Where?	Public access and highway	Public access and open air – note trespassory assembly.
Can conditions attach?	Yes – Section 12 Serious public disorder, serious damage to property, or serious disruption to the life of the community. Section 12 aa and ab – noise generation may result in serious disruption to organisations and persons.	Yes – Section 14 Serious public disorder, serious damage to property, or serious disruption to the life of the community. Section 14 aa and ab – noise generation may result in serious disruption to organisations and persons.
What conditions may be imposed?	Conditions as to the route of the procession or prohibiting it from entering any public place.	Conditions as to place at which the assembly may be (or continue to be) held, its maximum duration, or the maximum number of persons who may constitute it.
Minimum number of people?	No minimum requirement	Minimum of two people – although note section 14ZA and a one-person protest.
Can it be statutorily banned?	Three months, by the local council (Chief of Police in London), after consent from the Secretary of State has been sought.	No power.
Can legality of police conditions/ bans be questioned?	Yes, via judicial review.	Yes, via judicial review.

chief of police possesses powers by virtue of section 14A to apply for an order from the local authority/council, which prohibits the trespassory assembly.

It is important to note that there must be 20 or more persons on the land (open air) in question, and in addition to the trespassory assembly it must be reasonably believed that the trespassory assembly is:

- Being held without the requisite permission of the occupier, or is conducted in a manner that is likely to exceed the limits of any permission (Section 14A(1)(a));
- May result in serious disruption to the life of the community (Section 14A(1)(b)(i);
- Where the land or building or monument is of significant importance and there is a likelihood of significant damage to the land, building, or monument (Section 14A(1)(b)(ii)).[6]

  In *DPP v Jones (Margaret) and Another* [1999] 2 AC 240; [1999] 2 WLR 625 a 'trespassory assembly' undertaken on a public highway where there was an order in place, prohibiting the same, was not considered to be unlawful, and appeals against convictions were allowed.[7]

  > In my opinion the law would be left in an unsatisfactory state if your Lordships' House held that in this case the peaceful assembly on the highway, which caused no actual obstruction to persons passing along the highway, constituted a criminal trespass under section 14B because the assembly was not incidental to passage along the highway.[8]*Ibid.*

It is important to note that any order that is to be put in place for trespassory assemblies by the local authority/council will require consent from the Secretary of State.

Section 14B provides guidance on the requisite offences that will be committed in the event a trespassory assembly is arranged in contravention of an order that has been issued prohibiting such an assembly.

Section 14C provides the police with powers to stop a person that they reasonably believe may be heading to a trespassory assembly that has been prohibited, then they may stop and direct them elsewhere. A failure to comply will result in an individual being guilty of an offence.

6.4 Breach of the Peace

Under the common law, police (and local citizens) retain powers to arrest an individual for breach of the peace. They allow the police to wield many powers of arrest that they possess statutorily.

7 Where the land, or a building or monument on it, is of historical, architectural, archaeological or scientific importance, in significant damage to the land, building or monument.

8 Per Lord Hutton – 'However, I consider that there are indications in the authorities that the public's right to use the highway may be extended and I consider that the important issue before your Lordships' House is whether that right should be extended so that the public has a right in some circumstances to hold a peaceful assembly on the public highway provided that it does not obstruct the use of the highway'.

Interestingly, such an arrest for breach of the peace is *not* a criminal offence, in the normal sense of the term. The arrest can be made in order to deal with a breach of the peace or prevent a breach of the peace from taking place. It is important to note that a breach of the peace, while not a criminal offence, does generate police powers such as the power to arrest, the power to detain, the power to enter private premises, the power to disperse an assembly, and even the power to prevent people travelling. These common law powers allow the police to keep the peace and can be used in a variety of situations frequently where large crowds have gathered (or are going to gather) and there may be a threat of harm (immediate or imminent), such as assemblies, processions, rival sports fans, and public meetings. These powers can be utilised to keep the peace and disperse crowds legally.

6.4.1 Scope of Powers

A breach of the peace is said to occur 'whenever harm is actually done or is likely to be done to a person or, in his presence, to his property, or where a person is in fear of being harmed through an assault, affray, riot, unlawful assembly or other disturbance'.[9]

Thus, a police officer has the power to make an arrest for breach of the peace in three situations:

- A breach of the peace is committed and ongoing.
- A breach of the peace has occurred, and a further breach of the peace is threatened.
- There is a reasonable apprehension that a breach of the peace will be committed imminently.

It is important to note that in the event there is a reasonable belief of a breach of the peace in the immediate future, an individual can be reasonably apprehended in the interests of preventative action. This is an objective test. In *Duncan v Jones* [1936] 1 KB 218 and *Moss v McLachlan* [1985] IRLR 76; [1985] WLUK 376, during the miner's strikes, the police reasonably apprehended miners who they believed were looking to take part in strikes and were travelling to the pickets. They believed that allowing them to continue would lead to violent clashes between working and striking miners. As such, they went on to create a roadblock in order to prevent a breach of the peace and notified the vehicles – especially those that they believed contained miners who were striking – that failure to turn back and to proceed beyond the roadblock would lead to an arrest.

This has also led to further development of the law regarding the requirement of immediate/imminent threat, and that there is no legal requirement for breach of the peace to occur in the presence of a police officer. As such, they may act even

9 *R v Howell* [1982] QB 416, per Lord Justice Watkins at para 427.

before any breach of the peace occurs, as long as the arrest and the apprehended breach is not too remote, and there was a close proximity (*Moss v McLachlan* [1985] IRLR 76. This was further developed in the case of *R (Laporte) v Chief Constable of Gloucester* [2006] UKHL 55 where breach of the peace had to be sufficiently imminent, and any preventive action had to also be proportionate in response to the apprehension of imminent breach.

6.4.2 How Is Breach of the Peace Enforced?

It was discussed in 6.4 that an arrest for breach of the peace is not a criminal offence, although there are clear powers of arrest and detention. It may be that the police, having arrested and detained an individual, may release them without a charge.

Arrests for breach of the peace can lead to an individual being 'bound over' to maintain the peace. By binding an individual over, its goal is to keep the individual from breaching the peace following the court being satisfied that a breach of the peace involving violence or threat of violence has occurred, and that there remains a real risk of violence (or threat of) in the future. The Magistrates' Court or Crown Court may order the individual to refrain from engaging in certain activities, failing which they will pay a specified sum. A failure to comply with the order will result in a forfeiture of the sum. It is important to note that section 115 of the Magistrates' Courts Act denotes that bind over proceedings are civil but do require the criminal standard of proof.[10]

Breach of the peace can also lead to charges relating to obstructing a police officer in the execution of his duty under section 89(2) of the Police Act 1996.[11]

6.4.3 Breach of the Peace and Human Rights

There are some very clear concerns with powers that derive from breach of the peace and the fundamental rights that have been granted to individuals by the European Convention on Human Rights. Rights such as those that are guaranteed under Article 5 right to liberty and security, Article 10 freedom of speech, and Article 11 freedom of assembly are often cited as being in conflict with breach of the peace police powers. It is important to note that the common law powers of breach of the peace *has* been confirmed by the European Court of Human Rights as having a legal basis when considering the test regarding interference with convention rights.[12]

10 *Percy v Director of Public Prosecutions* [1995] 1 WLR 1382; [1995] 3 All ER 124.
11 *Duncan v Jones* [1936] 1 KB 218.
12 *Steel v United Kingdom* [1998] 28 EHRR 603.

R (Laporte) v Chief Constable of Gloucester *[2006] UKHL 55*

Case Facts

The facts involved three coaches that were travelling from London to protest at an RAF base in Gloucestershire, where many of the bombers used in the Iraq war were situated. The base, RAF Fairford, had already had a number of protests and demonstrations having taken place in its vicinity.

The three coaches were intercepted and searched using police powers derived from the Criminal Justice and Public Order Act 1994 and having found a mixture of items in their searches, including some that were suggestive of violence, at which point all three coaches were duly turned around and sent back to London with escorts. They were not allowed to stop at service stations for comfort breaks. The applicant sought to judicially review of the legality of the Chief Constable's decision in light of the interference with her rights of liberty and security by being detained on the coach, freedom of expression and freedom of assembly, and whether such a response was prescribed by law and necessary in a democratic society.

The House of Lords agreed, dismissing the Chief Constable's appeal, stating that the Chief Constable's response was disproportionate and indiscriminate. With regards to the legitimate aim of preventing a public disorder, it was accepted at the time of searching the coaches that there was no imminent breach of the peace. At paragraph 141 of the judgment, it was noted:

> I regard the reasonable apprehension of an imminent breach of the peace as an important threshold requirement, which must exist before any form of preventive action is permissible at common law. Where a reasonable apprehension of an imminent breach of the peace exists, then the preventive action taken must be reasonable or proportionate. But the threshold for preventive action is neither a broad test of reasonableness nor flexible.

KETTLING

Another case that demonstrates conflict between powers under breach of the peace and convention rights is the practice of 'kettling'. Here, containment strategies utilised by the police to control crowds has also been deemed as *not* amounting to a deprivation of liberty in breach of Article 5.

Austin and Others v United Kingdom *[2012] EHRR 14; [2012] ECHR 459*

Kettling containment strategies utilised within a police cordon for several hours was not a breach of Article 5 rights. The European Court of Human Rights agreed that the method of containment used was the most effective and the least intrusive, taking into account the context and the action, based upon the facts of the case.

Please revert back to our discussion on qualified rights at 5.4.3, where the courts are under a duty to ensure that a balance exists between giving effect to convention rights, and in the case of breach of the peace, allowing the police to stop a breach of the peace taking place.

6.5 Other Public Order Offences

We have covered in some detail some statutory public order offences, especially those that are linked to processions, assemblies, and the common law provision of breach of the peace, involving larger numbers, and the powers to disperse.

However, the Public Order Act 1986 also sought to control and maintain public order in general after the troubles in the 1980s. This included troubles of note, not just the miner's strikes, but also the Brixton riots, Toxteth riots, Moss Side riots, and the growth of football hooliganism and crowd trouble.

The offences created were riot, violent disorder, affray, fear or provocation of violence, harassment alarm, or distress. Let's consider these next.

6.5.1 Riot

Riot was the most serious of new offences introduced by the Public Order Act 1986. Riot is described as where 12 or more people that are present together use or threaten unlawful violence for a common purpose. In addition, the conduct (taken together) is such as would cause a person of reasonable firmness present at the scene to fear for their personal safety.

The definition is broken down in Figure 6.1:

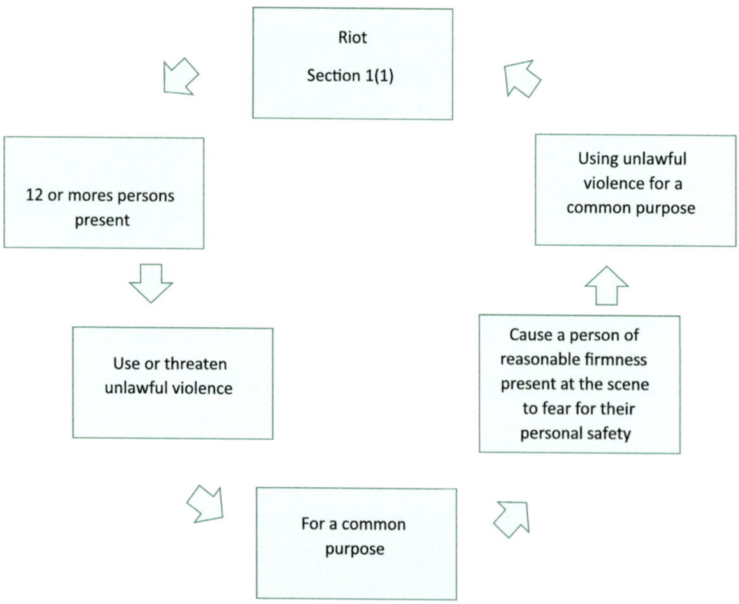

Figure 6.1 The legal definition of riot

All the elements in the definition must be proved in order to find a person guilty of riot. The violence deployed must be unlawful and offences of riot are triable only on indictment.

6.5.2 Violent Disorder

Violent disorder possesses similar requirements to that of riot, but requires only three people to be present, and is seen in section 2 of the Public Order Act 1986. The offence is triable either way, and it must be proved that the three or more persons who are present together used or threatened unlawful violence, and the conduct of the individuals causes a person of reasonable firmness to fear for their own personal safety. The offence is punishable by a maximum prison sentence of five years.

Some examples can be seen in table 6.2.

6.5.3 Affray

Another offence that forms part of the public order offences is that of Affray, which can be found in section 3 of the Public Order Act 1986. Here, a person will be guilty of an offence if they use or threaten to utilise unlawful violence which

Table 6.2 A table showcasing scenarios where violent disorder could apply

Example	Potential Outcomes
After attending a political protest and having been dispersed by the police, eight protesters search for counter protesters to fight. The protesters are seen shouting at the counter protesters across the street and threaten with violence. They then start to throw objects at the counter protesters. All eight are arrested after being seen by the police.	Falls short of riot under section 1 but could be prosecuted under section 2 of violent disorder. The offence has been committed in a public place (although it is irrelevant as to whether it is a public or private place), and the perpetrators were all threatening violence simultaneously.
Of the eight protesters, only two shouted and threatened violence simultaneously. Only one threw the object. The other five simply laughed and goaded.	It is immaterial as per section 2(2) whether or not the three or more people use or threaten unlawful violence simultaneously. R v NW [2010] EWCA Crim 404 – 'present together' does not require co-operation with those who are threatening violence.
Upon noticing the police, all eight run away, and after a short pursuit, two of the protesters are arrested, while six escaped.	It is important to note that not all the defendants have to be charged in order for there to be a successful prosecution. It needs to be made clear that the charged was one of the three (or two of the eight in our example) R v Mahroof (1988) 88 Cr App R 317

would cause a person of reasonable firmness to fear for their personal safety. It is important to note that in the event there are two or more people, their conduct as taken together will be considered. Furthermore, a threat of violence cannot be made by the use of words alone, as per subsection 3, and violence must be against a person and not property, as per section 8(a).

There is a very clear focus on the impact the affray would have on the reasonable bystander as opposed to the 'victim' involved. This is to ensure that public order is not only maintained, but appropriate sanctions are handed down to those who use violence (or the threat) of to cause fear to the public. If it cannot be proved that a person of reasonable firmness would not be in fear of their safety, then alternative charges that are more appropriate would be sought.

6.5.4 Fear or Provocation of Violence

This section of the Public Order Act is split into two separate facets. Section 4A was inserted by the Criminal Justice and Public Order Act 1994.

Section 4 of the act focusses on the use of threatening, abusive, and/or insulting words or behaviour towards another or distributes to another writing, sign, or visible representation which is also threatening, abusive, or insulting.

Again, there is a requirement that:

- There is a belief of immediate unlawful violence to the person.
- Provoke unlawful violence as a response from the person.
- There is a belief that unlawful violence will be used against the person.
- There is a belief that unlawful violence will be provoked from the person.

Section 4A of the Public Order Act focusses the offence against a specified victim, with a focus on intentional harassment, alarm, or distress. Here, the requirement is that the use of threatening, abusive, insulting words or behaviour/disorderly behaviour, or the display of any writing, sign, or visible representation which is also threatening or abusing causes another person harassment, alarm, or distress.

Section 4A also possesses a defence, if it can be shown that their conduct was reasonable.

6.5.5 Harassment, Alarm, or Distress

Section 5 of the act provides an offence (a) when a person uses threatening or abusive words or behaviour or disorderly behaviour, or (b) displays any writing, sign, or other visible representation which is threatening or abusive.

The previous has to be done within the hearing or sight of a person likely to be caused harassment, alarm, or distress. This is a key element, and is a question of fact, to be decided by the court, and can include police officers, who were not immune to being caused harassment, alarm, or distress.

See *DPP v Orum* (1989) Cr App R 261; [1989] 1 WLR 88. See also *Southard v Director of Public Prosecutions* [2006] EWHC 3449 (Admin), where use of the words 'fuck off' and 'fuck you' towards a police officer who was attempting to detain a suspect, while borderline, did amount to harassment.[13]

Section 5(2) provide that the act is applicable publicly and privately, with the exception of a dwelling.

This act also provides a defence, whereby an accused will need to prove:

- There was no reason to believe that was any person within hearing or sight who was likely to be caused harassment, alarm, or distress; or
- That he was inside a dwelling and had no reason to believe that the words or behaviour used, or the writing, sign, or other visible representation displayed, would be heard or seen by a person outside that or any other dwelling; or
- That his conduct was reasonable.

Chapter 6 Revision Points

- Laws in relation to public order is maintained by the police in order to ensure the safety of citizens.
- The Public Order Act 1986 provides the necessary statutory provisions with regards to public processions, assemblies, and public order in general.
- Articles 10 and 11 of the European Convention on Human Rights can conflict with the Public Order Act 1986, especially when conditions and bans are attached to processions and assemblies.
- Riot, violent disorder, and affray must consist of violence or the threat of violence but require minimum numbers before a charge can be brought. That is, 12 or more for riot, three or more for violent disorder, and two or more for affray.
- Breach of the peace is a common law provision unaffected by the Public Order Act 1986, which allows the police (or a citizen) to take preventative measures in maintaining peace and preventing a breach/imminent breach.
- Trespassory assemblies can be banned by the local authority after consent has been sought from the Secretary of State.

13 Per Mr Justice Fulford at para 24 and 25: 'Although officers are undoubtedly expected to be stoical, I do not consider that provides any real assistance to the appellant on the facts of this case. The abusive words were directed by the appellant at a police officer during an incident in which for a period he was making it impossible for the officer to detain a suspect. In those circumstances, however phlegmatic the officer may have been, it was a sustainable decision that a likely effect was to cause him some real harassment'

On the subject of the appellant's intention, he directed his words deliberately at the officer. Although his principal purpose may have been to stop the officer dealing with his brother, given the clear significance and meaning of the words 'fuck off' or 'fuck you', the court was, in my judgment, entitled to conclude that he intended to abuse the officer or was aware that his words may have that effect.

Multiple Choice Questions

Question 1

Two men are arguing about a parking spot and then start to fight each other. A young mother walking past with a pram asks them to stop. When they do not, she contacts the police, who attend and arrest both men.

Which offence has been committed by the men?

A. Riot.
B. Violent Disorder.
C. Affray.
D. Fear of provocation of violence.
E. Harassment, alarm, or distress.

Question 2

The local police have been notified of a procession in relation to the government's foreign policy that is taking place in a very busy town centre in the north-west. The date of the procession is on the same date that the local police will also be dealing with the effects of public sector strikes amongst health care staff, with many spending time keeping an eye on vulnerable patients and mentally ill patients in A&E. Having reviewed the availability of officers, the resources required to effectively and safely police the procession will not be enough, and the senior officer is concerned that some significant problems for the public may materialise with a very limited police presence and the subject matter of the procession. In the past, processions on government foreign policy has led to many arrests due to likelihood of counter protesters.

Which would be the best option for the police at this stage?

A. The senior police officer should allow the procession to go ahead, notwithstanding his concerns, and then ask the few police officers that he does have to immediately disperse the procession when it starts using breach of the peace powers.
B. The Commissioner of Police for the Metropolis should apply to the local authority for an order to prohibit the procession, who will then need to gain consent from the Secretary of State.
C. The Chief Officer of police should apply to the local district council for an order to prohibit the procession, who will then need to gain consent from the Secretary of State.

Question 2 (Continued)

D. The senior officer can provide notification to the organiser of the protest prohibiting the procession from going ahead.
E. The banning of the procession is not possible as this would be contrary to Articles 10 and 11 of the European Convention on Human Rights.

Question 3

A man is asked to wait inside a police cordon due to disruption that had been caused by a public assembly 500 yards up the street. The police explains that the assembly had become violent, and the containment was for their own safety. The man refused to wait and tried to force his way out and make his way towards the assembly, at which point he was arrested.

What is the current legal position?

A. An arrest can be made for obstructing a highway.
B. An arrest can be made for fear of provocation of violence.
C. An arrest can be made for harassment, alarm, or distress.
D. Article 5 of European Convention on Human Rights prohibits the deprivation of the man's liberty, and the police had to let him go about his business.
E. An arrest can be made for breach of the peace.

7 The Place of EU Law in the UK Constitution

7.1 SQE Syllabus

For SQE1, you will need to have an understanding of the place of EU law within the UK constitution now that the UK is no longer a member of the EU. Accordingly, an understanding of the Retained EU Law (Revocation and Reform) Act 2023 will be required.

7.2 Chapter Overview

The chapter will provide an overview of the place of EU law within the United Kingdom constitution post 'Brexit'. To that end, for context and understanding, we will cover some of the historical significance of EU law and its impact on the jurisdiction, and how that was impacted once the country had exited the Union. We will consider the impact of EU law in general, the withdrawal agreement, and as of 1 January 2024, 'assimilated law'.

7.3 The European Union

It may be beneficial for you to have an overview of the European Union and its modus operandi to have an understanding of the impact of the withdrawal from the European Union. *This area will not be assessed via SQE1*.

The European Union is a unique partnership between 27 European countries, known as Member States or EU countries. Together they cover much of the European continent. The EU is home to around 447 million people, which is around 6% of the world's population. Citizens of the EU countries are also EU citizens. It has its own legal order, which is independent of national law, and retains supremacy over national law in EU related matters.

The EU has a unique institutional structure, and this constantly evolves and develops to meet the needs of the EU and the European people. The structure features seven European institutions, seven EU bodies, and over 30 decentralised agencies that are located across the EU. There are also a further 20 EU agencies

DOI: 10.4324/9781032642024-13

and organisations that hold specific legal functions and four interinstitutional agencies that have been established to support the wide range of institutions.

All of these various establishments have defined roles which vary from the development of EU law and policy through to the implementation of policies and work within specialist areas such as transport, environment, and health.

There are four main decision-making institutions which lead the EU's administration, providing policy direction and specific roles within the lawmaking process. These are:

- The European Parliament
- The European Council
- The Council of the European Union
- The European Commission

The work of the four main institutions is then supported by bodies such as:

- The Court of Justice of the European Union
- The European Central Bank
- The European Court of Auditors

In addition, the remaining bodies and institutions then work to translate overarching policy to real action on the ground.

The Treaty of Rome in 1957 created the European Economic Community and the European Atomic Energy Company – this was named the European Union in 1992. The United Kingdom joined the EU in 1973, following the enactment of the European Communities Act 1972, which provided the necessary authority for EU law to be adopted.

Sources of EU Law

Domestic law generates EU law from five different sources. These are treaties, regulations, directives, decisions, and opinions/recommendations. *It is important to note that these are no longer applicable to the UK constitution and are not required for SQE1, but they do provide an effective review of how the previous arrangements worked.*

Table 7.1 provides a summary of the five sources:

Table 7.1 A table showcasing the sources of European Union Law

Treaties	Akin to primary legislation of the European Union.	Directly applicable and is highest form of EU law.
Regulations	Binding legislative acts, applied uniformly across the European Union.	Directly applicable, originates from the treaties.

(Continued)

Table 7.1 Continued

Directives	These are legal alterations that all EU members are required to achieve.	Not directly applicable but must be given effect nationally via a country's own legislative process.
Decisions	Binding decisions aimed specifically at those it addresses.	Directly applicable
Recommendations/ Opinions	Non-binding and imposes no legal obligations.	Non-binding.

When the UK joined the EU, by virtue of the European Communities Act 1972, it became the established approach that the courts would interpret law with a view to compliance with Community law. However, if there was a conflict between the national law and Community law, there was a requirement to give precedence to Community law given its superiority.

The key case that considered this view was the landmark decision in *R (Factortame Ltd) (no2) v Secretary of State for Transport* [1991] 1 AC 603.

In the case, there existed a conflict between Community law and the national law in the form of the Merchant Shipping Act 1988. Community law prevailed and the act was disapplied, allowing the grant of interim relief. This was the first time in the United Kingdom's constitutional history that an Act of Parliament had been disapplied by a national court. This led to much academic debate and discussion around the doctrine of the supremacy of Parliament.

7.4 'Brexit' and the Relationship Between the UK and the EU

The United Kingdom left the European Union at 11:00 pm on 31 January 2020. This came about by virtue of the EU Referendum Act 2015, which had provided the government with the ability to call for a referendum on the UK's continued membership.

At the time, there had been a number of disagreements between the EU and the UK on subjects ranging from beef and chocolate through to issues with migration and economic unrest. The proposal for a series of measures that would have weakened Britain's financial sector led to then Prime Minister David Cameron vetoing an EU treaty – the first Prime Minister to take this step.

In early 2013, the Prime Minister spoke on the need to renegotiate membership of the EU and this became part of the platform leading up to the next general election. After winning the election in May 2015, Cameron started the process of renegotiating the terms of the relationship between the UK and the EU. This focussed on concerns regarding migration, migrant welfare payments, financial safeguards, and a means to allow EU regulations to be blocked by the UK. Ultimately, he was unsuccessful in gaining concessions from the EU and in February 2016, he set the date of the referendum as 23 June of that year.

On the date of the referendum, 71.8% of the population turned out to cast their vote with the referendum passing with a slim majority of 51.9% to 48.1%. This result was despite all of the major political parties seeking to reinforce the view that leaving the EU was not the preferred option. This support for remaining within the EU led to David Cameron resigning as Prime Minister in the wake of the result.

It is also important to note that there were stark differences in the views taken across the nations of the United Kingdom, with Northern Ireland and Scotland both voting to remain – in Scotland's case by a significant majority of 62% to 38%.

There then followed a period of significant turmoil as the ruling party often wrestled with itself over how best to enact the will of the British people. The matter of withdrawal from the EU was even contested in court, as it was believed that royal prerogative powers could be utilised to withdraw the country from the EU.

However, in the Supreme Court matter of *R(Miller) v Secretary of State for Exiting the European Union* [2017] UKSC 5, it was decided that the powers to notify the European Union of withdrawal had to be triggered by Parliament and not the royal prerogative, as such a withdrawal would lead to a change in the constitutional position of the country with respect to the rights and freedoms enjoyed by citizens. This led to the enactment of the EU (Notification of Withdrawal) Act 2017.

The European Union (Withdrawal) Act 2018 and the European Union (Withdrawal Agreement) Act 2020 followed to formally withdraw the United Kingdom from the European Union.

7.5 The Withdrawal Agreement and the Future Jurisdiction of the Court of Justice of the European Union

The withdrawal agreement between the UK and EU seeks to govern the concept of EU–UK relations within the UK constitution after the exit. The agreement consists of six parts and 185 articles, which demonstrates the impact of what membership of the European Union entailed and how difficult it has become to separate such a relationship.

Furthermore, it provides clarity of the future place of EU law within the UK constitution.

The withdrawal agreement and other separation agreements have a special status, not simply through the transition period, but also beyond in areas such as citizens' rights (Part 2), separations issues (Part 3) and the Northern Ireland Protocol.

To that effect, it is important to note that the Court of Justice of the European Union could still play a role within the UK constitution with respect to the withdrawal agreement.

In relation to Part 2 of the withdrawal agreement, preliminary references must be allowed for a period of up to eight years after the transition period. It is also stated within Article 86 of the withdrawal agreement that decisions delivered by the Court of Justice of the European Union after the transition period will continue to have jurisdiction if any preliminary references were raised before the end of the transition period.[1]

Similarly, on the question of the Northern Ireland Protocol, the Court of Justice of the European Union will have similar powers to that of when the UK was an EU member,. thus allowing the European Commission to initiate proceedings should legal issues arise in relation to the protocol. The UK courts will also be bound by case law derived from the Court of Justice of the European Union (in Northern Ireland Protocol issues) – not simply required to 'have regard' to the same.[2]

The whole process has therefore moved to a position where compatibility of domestic law with the withdrawal agreement (and by extension EU law) is paramount, and this is given effect under section 7A (1, 2, and 3) of the European Union (Withdrawal) Act 2018.

7.6 The Position of EU Law Within the United Kingdom Constitution

In order to understand the current position of EU law within the UK constitution, it is important to understand the initial changes that were brought about by 2018

1 *The Commissioners for Her Majesty's Revenue and Customs v Martyn Glen Perfect* [2022] EWCA Civ 330, at paragraphs 13 and 16 'As a result of the United Kingdom's withdrawal from the EU, Courts in this jurisdiction are not generally bound by decisions of the CJEU made after 31 December 2020: see section 6(1) of the European Union (Withdrawal) Act 2018 ("the 2018 Act"). Section 6(2) of that Act states that a Court "may have regard" to such decisions'.

It follows that, under the terms of the Withdrawal Agreement, judgments of the CJEU on references from United Kingdom Courts and Tribunals made before the end of 2020 are to have 'binding force in their entirety on and in the United Kingdom' even if handed down in 2021 or later. Further, the United Kingdom is required by article 4(2) to ensure compliance with article 4(1) 'through domestic primary legislation'.

2 See Articles 4(4) and 4(5) of the Withdrawal Agreement.

Withdrawal Act and the development of those changes through the 2023 Reform Act.

The European Union (Withdrawal) Act 2018

The 2018 Withdrawal Act made three critical changes:

- It repealed the European Communities Act 1972 on exit day, and thus put an end to the EU's legislative capacity over the United Kingdom.
- It created a new source of 'retained' EU law, which was a snapshot of EU law prior to the exiting the EU.
- It provided wide powers for the executive and devolved administrations to make any changes to 'retained' EU law that was going to be problematic. These are also known as 'Henry VIII' clauses.

The Retained EU Law (Revocation and Reform) Act 2023

The 2023 Reform Act has made a number of critical changes:

- It repeals the principle of supremacy of EU law from UK law by the end of 2023;
- It facilitates domestic courts departing from retained case law;
- It repeals directly effective EU law rights and obligations in UK law by the end of 2023;
- It abolished general principles of EU law in UK law by the end of 2023;
- It introduced a new 'assimilated' law, which would replace 'retained' EU law.

In essence, the place of EU law within the UK constitution is now extremely limited. The act allows for retained EU law to be given effect in a manner that is compatible with domestic law.

Table 7.2 documents the present position:

Table 7.2 The current position of assimilated law in the UK

Retained EU Law (Revocation and Reform) Act 2023	
Section 2	**Repeals section 4 of the European Union (Withdrawal) Act 2018.** Anything which, immediately before the end of 2023, is retained EU law by virtue of that section is not recognised or available in domestic law at or after that time (and, accordingly, is not to be enforced, allowed, or followed).
Section 3	**Abolishes the Supremacy of EU law. Inserts into section 5 of the European Union (Withdrawal) Act 2018** A1 – **The principle of the supremacy of EU law is not part of domestic law.**

(Continued)

Table 7.2 Continued

Retained EU Law (Revocation and Reform) Act 2023	
	This applies after the end of 2023, in relation to any enactment or rule of law (whenever passed or made). A2 – Any provision of retained direct EU legislation – (a) must, so far as possible, be read and given effect in a way which is **compatible with all domestic enactments**, and (b) is subject to all domestic enactments, so far as it is incompatible with them.
Section 4	**Abolished General Principles of EU law.** Inserts into section 5 of the European Union (Withdrawal) Act 2018 A4 – No general principle of EU law is part of domestic law after the end of 2023.
Section 5	**Introduces 'Assimilated law'** Outlines terms containing 'Retained' would be amended to 'Assimilated' after end of 2023. For example: Retained EU law → Assimilated law. Retained Direct EU legislation → Assimilated direct legislation. Retained EU Obligation → Assimilated obligation. Retained EU case law – Assimilated EU case law.
Section 6 – *****This version is prospective***** Was not in force at the time of Royal Assent in June 2023, see section 22(3) of the act.	**Role of the Courts** Provides guidance on the role of the national courts in the interpretation of 'retained' EU case law and when it (a higher court) can depart from a decision of the CJEU. Previously, this was when it appeared 'right to do so'. In deciding whether to depart from any retained EU case law the higher court concerned must (among other things) have regard to – (a) the fact that decisions of a foreign court are not (unless otherwise provided) binding; (b) any changes of circumstances which are relevant to the retained EU case law; (c) the extent to which the retained EU case law restricts the proper development of domestic law.

(Continued)

Table 7.2 Continued

Retained EU Law (Revocation and Reform) Act 2023	
	The section also allows for the higher courts to depart from domestic retained case law, that is, any decisions pertaining to the EU that were handed down domestically before 31 December 2020. A higher court may depart from its own retained domestic case law if it considers it right to do so having regard (among other things) to – (a) the extent to which the retained domestic case law is determined or influenced by retained EU case law from which the court has departed or would depart; (b) any changes of circumstances which are relevant to the retained domestic case law; (c) the extent to which the retained domestic case law restricts the proper development of domestic law.
Section 8	**Incompatibility Orders** Adds a new section into the European Union (Withdrawal) Act 2018 where the courts must make an incompatibility order when any retained direct EU legislation conflicts with domestic legislation by virtue of section 8(2). An incompatibility order may: (a) set out the effect of the relevant provision in its operation in relation to that particular case; (b) delay the coming into force of the order; (c) remove or limit any effect of the operation of the relevant provision before the coming into force of the order.

Chapter 7 Revision Points

- The UK has now left the European Union, and as such, European Union law no longer applies to UK law.
- UK domestic courts are not required to follow any decisions of the Court of Justice of the European Union.
- The principle of supremacy is no longer a part of domestic law.
- As of 1 January 2024, retained EU law is now to be deemed as 'assimilated law' as per the Retained EU Law (Revocation and Reform) Act 2023.
- The withdrawal agreement has a special status that allows for the withdrawal agreement to take precedence over domestic law including in some matters of EU.

Multiple Choice Questions

Question 1

You are acting on behalf of a client who is a Union citizen who has lived in the UK for eight years. You assess that the citizenship issue falls within Part 2 of the withdrawal agreement with the European Union.

Which best describes the current position?

A. The client cannot rely on EU law as he moved to the UK before the implementation period.
B. The client must rely on domestic law as the UK has now left the European Union.
C. The client can rely on the articles contained within the withdrawal agreement.
D. The client must rely on matters of retained EU law.
E. The client can rely on the EU law after making a reference to the Court of Justice of the European Union.

Question 2

Assimilated law was established by the Retained EU Law (Revocation and Reform) Act 2023, to given effect from 1 January 2024.

Which of the following statements in relation to the Retained EU Law (Revocation and Reform) Act 2023 is most accurate?

A. Supremacy of EU law retained in matters whereby the decision was made before implementation period.
B. Assimilated law is supreme over retained EU law.
C. Assimilated law must take precedence over national law, now that the 'retained EU law' element has been removed.
D. Abolishes the supremacy of EU law.
E. Assimilated law is a new source of EU law that needs to be given effect in national law.

Question 3

With respect to the future relationship between the national courts and the Court of Justice of the European Union, which statement is most accurate?

A. References to the Court of Justice of the European Union can be made when there is a lack of clarity regarding assimilated law by both the lower and the higher courts.
B. References to the Court of Justice of the European Union can be made when there is a lack of clarity regarding assimilated law by just the higher courts.
C. References made before the end of the implementation period and the subsequent D.
References can be made in very specific circumstances when matters involve the withdrawal agreement.
E. No references are permitted now that the UK has left the European Union.

8 Answers to Multiple Choice Questions

8.1 Chapter Overview

This chapter provides the answers to the multiple choice questions at the end of each part of the book.

DOI: 10.4324/9781032642024-14

8.2 Chapter 1 – Introduction to the United Kingdom Constitution

Question 1

Answer

Option B is correct. The introduction of a compensation scheme of this kind can be aligned with the setting up of the criminal injuries compensation scheme that was introduced using prerogative powers. However, any new scheme will require parliamentary approval for financial resource, as the government cannot use the prerogative to authorise expenditure.

Question 2

Answer

Option E is correct. The notion of parliamentary sovereignty will apply meaning that Parliament can pass any legislation it pleases. However, the courts will recognise the constitutional convention's existence, even though this will not prevent the application of the new law.

Question 3

Answer

Option D is correct as by constitutional convention any act that has progressed through all stages of Parliament will always be granted Royal Assent.

8.3 Chapter 2 – Constitutional Institutions and Roles

Question 1

Answer

Option E is correct. The Parliament Act 1949 allows the House of Lords to delay legislation for up to one year and they can force further scrutiny of the proposed legislation via proposed amendments. Ultimately, though, the Lords cannot prevent a bill from becoming law.

Question 2

Answer

Option B is correct. There exists a constitutional convention that the monarch's speech is drafted by the Prime Minister and is the King's requirement to follow the advice of his Prime Minister. It should be noted that a monarch can advise a minister of state on legislation.

Question 3

Answer

Option C is correct. Where a matter is covered by statute, the royal prerogative cannot be used against the will of Parliament.

8.4 Chapter 3 – Supremacy, the Rule of Law, and the Separation of Powers

Question 1

Answer

Option B is correct. The term the rule of law relates to the role that the law plays in the regulation of the powers of the state and how the liberties of private citizens are protected. The rule of law is a guiding principle for the courts, as they interpret law, and is codified in section 1 of the Constitutional Reform Act 2005.

Question 2

Answer

Option B is correct. A key aspect of the 'rule of law' doctrine is that we are all equal under the law. The exception would be if the law provided immunity, which is not the case here.

Question 3

Answer

Option C is correct. As she is a serving judge, she is statutorily disqualified from standing for election. Under the doctrine of 'the separation of powers', it is not permitted to hold positions within two different arms of the state. This is with a view to avoiding any danger of powers being abused.

8.5 Chapter 4 – Judicial Review and Access to the Courts

Question 1

Answer

Option B is correct. Analogous with the case of Vine v National Dock Labour Board [1957] A.C. 488. The licensing authority delegated powers in breach of the rule against delegation and neither of the two exemptions (neither civil servant nor local authority committee exemption) applied because the decision was delegated to the morality committee of the local church.

Question 2

Answer

Option A is correct. The ouster clause is unlikely to protect the decision from challenge as these clauses do not protect decisions that are nullities. However, the company is probably guilty of undue delay as they have waited for two months without good reason so will not be granted permission to bring a claim.

Question 3

Answer

Option B is correct. A mandatory order will force the council to consider the woman's application. Although the woman has lost money due to the refusal to consider the application, she is unlikely to obtain damages.

8.6 Chapter 5 – The Human Rights Act 1998

Question 1

Answer

Option C is correct. The Strasbourg court does have strict procedures, whereby it requires an application within four months of an applicant having exhausted all remedies in the state concerned prior to applying.

Question 2

Answer

Option C is correct. The courts have a duty to interpret the legislation by virtue of section 3 of the Human Rights Act 1998 in a manner that will allow it to comply with convention rights (so far as it is possible to do so). D is not correct as the court must seek to interpret as opposed to issuing a declaration of incompatibility immediately. A is not correct as the Human Rights Act provides the court the power to give effect to convention rights.

Question 3

Answer

Option A is correct. The act, as per sections 6(3), states a 'public authority' includes a court or tribunal, and any person certain of whose functions are functions of a public nature.

8.7 Chapter 6 – Public Order Law and Offences

Question 1

Answer

Option C is correct. Remember, affray requires a person to use (or threaten to use) unlawful violence towards another, which would cause a person of reasonable firmness present to fear for their personal safety. As such, we have the perpetrator, the 'victim', and a hypothetical bystander of reasonable firmness who may fear for her safety, especially as she is pushing a pram. Remember that for riot and violent disorder, there is a requirement that 12 or more for riot and three or more for violent disorder. D and E would not be applicable as these are lesser offences.

Question 2

Answer

Option C is correct. The best option would be to prohibit the protest given the lack of resources needed to effectively and safely police the protest. The question denotes that the procession is in the north-west, and as such B, with the Commissioner of Police for the Metropolis, would not apply. Even if the procession was in London, this would be incorrect as the Commissioner of Police for the Metropolis simply needs consent from the Secretary of State. D cannot apply, as permission to prohibit needs to be sought from the local district council, who in turn require the consent of the Secretary of State. With regards to A, the local police could allow the protest to go ahead, however they will not be able to use breach of the peace powers unless there is an imminent breach. In the event that they utilise these powers to disperse without satisfying the requirements, then this will be an act of ultra vires and an abuse of police powers.

Question 3

Answer

Option E is correct. The police can arrest him for breach of the peace as a preventative measure, especially as it is apparent that the assembly up the road, where he seems to be heading, has become violent. D would not be applicable as containment strategies have been decided to not always infringe rights under Article 5, although in the event of any subsequent claim, the circumstances will be carefully considered by the court. A would not apply as he is not obstructing the highway, and B and C would not be applicable as these are public order offences whereby the man must use towards another person threatening, abusive, or insulting words or behaviour, and for harassment, alarm, or distress the man must use threatening (or abusive) words or behaviour, or disorderly behaviour.

8.8 Chapter 7 – The Place of EU Law in the UK Constitution

Question 1

Answer

Option C is correct. The withdrawal agreement has a special status that does seek to guarantee citizens' rights. Accordingly, any issues that fall within the articles in Part 2 can be relied upon and enforced in a UK court of law.

Question 2

Answer

Option D is correct. In terms of the national law, the Retained EU Law (Revocation and Reform) Act 2023 was enacted to the detriment of retained EU law. The act seeks to ensure that domestic law now takes precedence over retained EU law.

Question 3

Answer

Option D is correct. The special nature of the withdrawal agreement continues to allow references to be made in very specific circumstances, such as that of the Northern Ireland Protocol citizens' rights and financial settlement matters, and any interpretation questions that arise thereof.

Index

For Product Safety Concerns and Information please contact our EU representative GPSR@taylorandfrancis.com Taylor & Francis Verlag GmbH, Kaufingerstraße 24, 80331 München, Germany